STO LAT:

A Modern Guide to Polish Genealogy

This book would never have left the draft stage had it not been for my good fortune in finding the most patient and wise editor in Hal Learman. He is an experienced genealogist who knows what researchers are looking for and how to guide them through the process. He embraced the book's concept and championed what I had to say and has been a partner in that process. If you find this book easy to read, free of unnecessary sentences, and generally in good order—thank Hal! I know I do.

The book cover was designed by artist Peg Pasternak, MFA, a graduate of Rhode Island School of Design and Parsons School of Design, New York. The documents in this collage represent Peg's heritage (her paternal line, Pasternak and Michalski; and her maternal line, Osip and Kudła). The flower intertwined into the artwork is called "Polish Spirit" and is a clematis developed by Brother Stefan Franczak from Jeziorna, Wieluń, Poland. Peg is an art teacher at Lahser High School in Bloomfield Hills, Michigan and a former student of the author, Cecile Wendt Jensen.

The layout and design of *STO LAT* is by consultant Chita Hunter—Hunter Designs, who also served as project manager. Chita graduated from Michigan's Lawrence Technological University with a Bachelor of Science Degree in Architecture. She is an architectural designer, a NCIDQ-certified Interior Designer, a software instructor, and an Adode Certified Expert in InDesign, Photoshop, Illustrator, and InCopy.

STO LAT:

A Modern Guide
to Polish Genealogy

Cecile Wendt Jensen

Copyright 2010
by
Cecile Wendt Jensen
ISBN 978-0-615-36099-7

Published by
Michigan Polonia, LLC
145 South Livernois Road #154
Rochester Hills, Michigan 48307
www.mipolonia.net

Printed in the
United States of America

Also By
Cecile Wendt Jensen:
Arcadia Publishing
Detroit's Polonia (2006)
Detroit's Mount Elliott Cemetery (2006)
Detroit's Mount Olivet Cemetery (2006)
www.arcadiapublishing.com

Second Printing

Table of Contents

Table of Contents

Table of Contents

Acknowledgements

I extend my appreciation to the following content developers who granted permission for the use of their work: Matthew Bielawa, Heinz Chinnow, The Church of Jesus Christ of Latter-day Saints, The Generations Network, Inc., William F. (Fred) Hoffman, Barabel Johnson, Joseph Martin, Stephen P. Morse, Mount Elliott Cemetery Association, Robert Tachna, Sonja Nishimoto, Kari Wood, and Bill Nichols, owner of Otto Schemansky and Sons Monuments, Detroit.

A special thank you to Thomas Phinney, Senior Product Manager, Font Solutions at Extensis. The body text of this book is set in Arno Pro, an Adobe Original typeface designed by Robert Slimbach.

Special thanks to my patient husband, James Jensen, who—being of Irish, French Canadian, and English heritage—never grumbles when he is served pierogi and sauerkraut.

I have dedicated this book to four special relatives who were my "informants" when I began our family research in the 1970s. "They knew the secrets and told the stories"—Lillian Ewald Lesinski (1897-1999), Katherine Wojtkowiak Topolewski (1893-1987), Walter Banoski (1929-), and Verna Harja Bivins (1918-2002).

Introduction:

STO LAT: A Modern Guide to Polish Genealogy

Sto lat! Sto lat! Niech żyje, żyje nam
(May you live a hundred years!)

-Polish celebration song

Sto Lat (Polish for one hundred years) is the title of a celebration song often sung on birthdays. This book offers a plan for gathering at least one hundred years of family records and is a compilation of research techniques I developed during my thirty years of teaching. These are tried and true techniques I use for my clients and patrons during my volunteer hours at the local Family History Center (FHC). I present both traditional and digital techniques. I answer common research questions and offer suggestions to help novices and advanced family historians find ancestors in North America and Poland. Congratulations on embarking on a fantastic journey! Documenting your family will call on all of your skills learned in high school, college, and the school of life; and will deliver an understanding, knowledge, and appreciation of your ancestors.

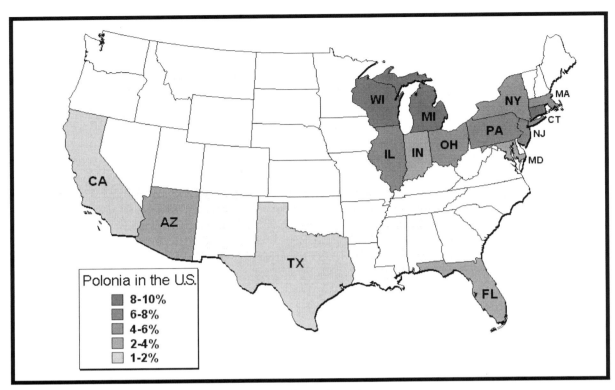

Polonia distribution by U.S. states.

Polish-American researchers are often unsure of how to start the research process and wonder if there are available records. But one visit to a Polish genealogical society meeting will dispel the myth that records were destroyed during the World Wars and that language barriers make research difficult. At any given meeting, members may be showing off the 1850 birth record they found on microfilm at the local Family History Center or displaying photos of their recent visit to their ancestral village in Poland. They might not be able to speak or read Polish; but that is okay.

Over the last twenty-five years, colleagues have been writing guide books and developing finding aids. Their work helps you locate the ancestral villages and decipher records written in Polish, German, Russian, and Latin. Books, CD's, maps, Web sites, and databases developed in North America and Poland support this effort. You are not alone in your research—there are many Polish-Americans (Pol-Ams)! The 2000 U.S. census recorded 10 million Americans with Polish ancestry. It is one of the top ten ethnicities in the U.S., sandwiched between Italian-Americans and French-Americans.

Now is a wonderful time to begin your Pol-Am research. Traditional resources stock the shelves of local and national libraries and the Internet offers new ways to research in both the United States and Poland.

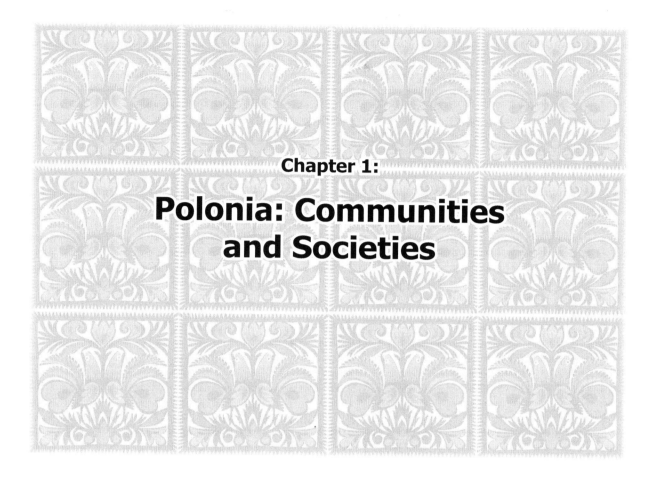

Chapter 1:
Polonia: Communities and Societies

O ne of the first guidelines family genealogists learn in the research process is to start with the ancestors you know and work your way back, generation by generation. With that in mind, we need to explore "Polonia", a term for descendants of Poles who live outside of Poland. After identifying the Polonian community of your ancestors, you will begin to trace the path back to your Polish ancestral village.

This book includes sample documents for the immigrants who arrived during the mid-19th to mid-20th centuries. Their reasons for leaving their homeland varied. Some immigrants were recruited by companies looking for cheap labor; others heard about jobs from relatives who had already resettled in America. They created Polish-American colonies, establishing parishes with schools, benevolent societies, newspapers, and neighborhoods. Their legacies live on today whether their descendants live in the same area or have moved to other regions of the country.

Many of the Polonian communities have Polish Genealogical Societies (PGS). Large or small, they continue to encourage documentation of the early history of these communities. Your research will be enriched if you join a society. You might even find a cousin or two.

Many of the founders of the American Polish genealogy societies descended from parents or grandparents born in Poland. They attended bilingual parish schools in the U.S. and were fluent in both Polish and English. Because "baby boomers" and their children may have only one line that hails from Poland, they may have never heard Polish spoken at home. This is another benefit of joining a society. There are always members who still speak Polish. The societies are a mix of the original Polish descendants and Pol-Ams who have moved into the area. Some even have ties with the recent immigrants who arrived after the Solidarity Movement of the 1980s. Membership in these societies gives depth to your research. Materials held by genealogical societies may never become part of an online database or public archive. This grass roots research is priceless. Who knows, the local PGS may have a grade school ledger from 1899 or a *pamiątka* (memento) that is the key you need in your research.

What do Polish Genealogy Societies offer?

If you Google "Polish Genealogy Society" the first hit is **The Polish Genealogical Society of America (PGSA)**. Founded in Chicago in 1978, the society has broad interests. Its mission is to collect, disseminate, and preserve information on Polish and Polish-American family history and to help its members in their own research. The society has published books, CD's, and online resources that benefit Pol-Ams across the nation. Their yearly conference features speakers from the U.S. and Poland. *Rodziny*, the society's journal, offers informative articles illustrated with maps and photos. PGSA volunteers offer weekly assistance at The Polish Museum and Library. *www.pgsa.org*

The 2000 U.S. census recorded 496,273 Californians with Polish heritage. **The Polish Genealogical Society of California (PGS-CA)** was founded in 1989 to serve this population, to promote the research of Polish family heritage, and to provide a forum for members to learn how to research their ancestral lines. *The PGSC Bulletin* is their quarterly publication. Their resource collection is housed at the Los Angeles Family History Center (LAFHC). PGS-CA has been instrumental in organizing and hosting the biennial United Polish Genealogy Society Seminar held in Salt Lake City, Utah featuring research at the renowned Family History Library. *www.pgsca.org*

The Polish Genealogical Society of Greater Cleveland (PGSGC) was organized in 1991 to help members study their Polish ancestry, culture, and heritage. *Our Polish Ancestors* newsletter is published quarterly. Cleveland is home to the Pol-Am community known as Warszawa. *www.freewebs.com/pgsgc*

The Polish Genealogical Society of Connecticut and the Northeast, Inc. (PGSCTNE) promotes research in the Connecticut River Valley and parts of New England and Mid-Atlantic states of New York, New Jersey, Pennsylvania, Maryland, and Delaware. Their publication, *Pathways and Passages,* is a semi-annual newsletter. PGSCTNE's Web site hosts unique databases for the Polish villages of Dąbrowa Białostocka, Myszyniec, and Wola Raniżowska. *www.pgsctne.org*

The Polish Genealogical Society of Massachusetts (PGSMA) was founded in 1989. Their newsletter, *Biuletyn Korzenie (Roots Bulletin),* is published twice a year. Meetings with speakers are held throughout the year and the society's new home is at the Polish Center at Elms College in Chicopee, Massachusetts. *www.rootsweb.com/~mapgsm*

The Polish Genealogical Society of Michigan (PGSM), founded in 1979, is dedicated to encouraging research in Michigan Polonia—the third largest Pol-Am community in the U.S.—and in all regions of Poland. The society's journal, *The Polish Eaglet*, is published three times per year. Microfilmed records for the early Detroit Archdiocese Roman Catholic parishes are held at the Burton Collection at the Detroit Public Library. Monthly meetings and a yearly seminar offer opportunities to meet and share research. *www.pgsm.org*

The Polish Genealogical Society of Minnesota (PGSMN) issues a quarterly PGSMN newsletter. Their holdings are at the Minnesota Genealogical Library in Golden Valley, Minnesota, where their meetings are also held. They have expertise in Kashubian research and their Web site includes surnames being researched by members as well as a link to join their PGSMN mail list. *www.rootsweb.com/~mnpolgs/pgs-mn.html*

The Polish Genealogical Society of New York State (PGSNYS) was founded in 1988. The society publishes *Searchers* three times a year. Headquartered in Buffalo, their interests include promoting the study of Polish genealogy in western New York and southern Ontario, Canada. Their holdings are part of the Erie Public Library Collection. Visit the society Web site at: *www.pgsnys.org*

The Polish Genealogical Society of Texas (PGST), founded in 1982, publishes Polish-Texan research for previously undocumented and unexplored areas. They sponsor workshops on historical and genealogical topics relevant to Poles in Texas. Their Web site has a gallery of photos of Polish villages commissioned by society members. Online indexes include surnames and articles in their periodical, *Polish Footprints. www.pgst.org*

The PGS community welcomes the **Toledo Polish Genealogy Society (TPGS)**. Founded in 2004, their focus is to help genealogists who are researching ancestors in Poland or Polish-Americans in the Toledo, Ohio area. The Pol-Am community looks forward to learning about Toledo's two Polish enclaves, Kuschwantz and Lagrinka. *www.tpgs02.org*

What if my Polish ancestors were not Roman Catholic?

Jewish communities were largest in Russian and Austrian Poland; Mennonites in the Vistula Delta area; and the Lemkos inhabited the Lower Beskid range of the Carpathian Mountains. The following societies conduct research for minorities who lived in Poland:

The International Association of Jewish Genealogical Societies (IAJGS) coordinates the activities and annual conference of more than 75 national and local Jewish genealogical societies around the world. *www.iajgs.org*

The Society for German Genealogy in Eastern Europe (SGGEE) focuses on German ancestry generally of the Lutheran, Baptist, or Moravian faiths who lived in present-day Poland and northwestern Ukraine. *www.sggee.org*

The archives of the **Mennonite Heritage Centre (MHC)** include the records of the Prussian and Russian Mennonite community, as well as documents, personal papers, etc., of many individuals. *www.mennonitechurch.ca/programs/archives*

Lemko.org offers a wealth of information including a dictionary of Lemko surnames and an index to localities formerly inhabited by Lemkos prior to 1947. There are links to additional Lemko societies world wide. *www.lemko.org*

The partitions of Russian, Prussian, and Austrian Poland (1772-1918).

Chapter 2:
Foundation Research

The first step to finding your Polish ancestors starts here in the United States. The core records to look for are the U.S. census and naturalization papers. The U.S. census will pinpoint the date of arrival in the U.S. for the family members and state if the males held alien status or were naturalized. It will also offer the key to finding the region the family hailed from: German Poland, Russian Poland, or Austrian Poland (a.k.a. Galicia; see map on previous page). Poland was not on the map for 123 years and ethnic Poles carried papers stating they were subjects of the governing countries. The census, traditionally accessed on microfilm, is now online at fee-based Web sites.

If the census indicates your ancestor was naturalized, contact the local court or state archives for copies of their records. *The Red Book*, a staple of genealogy reference libraries, outlines where records are kept in each state and how to place an order. Many archives have Web sites with finding aids online. For example, Pennsylvania's naturalization papers are accessible for free. ***www.footnote.com***

I hope you share my commitment to making Polish genealogy as popular and easy to do as that of the English and the Germans. If so, you will want to be as accurate as possible with your research and cite your sources. If this sounds like a high school English term paper, there is good reason. You want your research to stand up to examination, with a paper trail for future researchers. Poland has a thousand years of rich history; but, Polonia's history is only about 150 years old in the U.S. Play a role in properly documenting your Polish immigrants.

As you begin your research, you will collect a bookshelf of materials created to help with this quest. I have compiled a list of the books on my Polonian shelf and it is no surprise that Rosemary A. Chorzempa's *Polish Roots* tops the list. For many of us, this was our first guide to Polish genealogy. My copy has sticky notes marking the lists of Saints' Feast Days that influenced naming patterns. Also flagged is the page instructing how to address a letter to Poland. The following list starts with my most dog-eared volumes. I grouped them into three categories and in the sequence that I use them.

What were my ancestors' Polish names?

This question needs to be answered before a successful search can begin. Grandpa might have been known as Tom Jepko here in the States; but, you need to know he was Tomasz Zdziebko in Poland. That is why *Polish Surnames: Origins and Meanings* by William F. Hoffman starts my list. The first half of the book consists of twelve chapters explaining the origins and meanings of Polish surnames and suggests how they developed and changed. The second half is an index of some 30,000 common surnames, organized by the roots they came from, with indications of how many Polish citizens bore each name as of 1990.

Once I have the surname straightened out, my next resource is *First Names of the Polish Commonwealth: Origins & Meanings* by William F. Hoffman and George W. Helon. It includes names of Czech, German, Greek, Hebrew, Hungarian, Latin, Lithuanian, Polish, Russian, Ukrainian, and Yiddish origin. This book saved me from entering duplicate ancestors in my database having read that Bogumiła and Gottliebia was the same name (one vital record was written in Polish and the other in German). Be sure to read the introduction for the historical and linguistic backgrounds. There are charts with the Polish, Hebrew, Russian Cyrillic, and Ukrainian Cyrillic alphabets, as well as a list of Cyrillic forms of common Jewish first names.

Where did they live?

Later, we will investigate ship manifests, naturalization documents, U.S. census records, draft cards, and Social Security applications for historic villages. But if you already know the European residence of your Polish ancestors, then you still need to find their place of worship in order to gather religious records. The Family History Library (FHL) catalog can help;

but, it does not always include the villages that correspond to the spiritual center. So, we can reach for Stanisław Litak's *The Latin Church in the Polish Commonwealth in 1772*. Using the maps and index of this book, you can pinpoint to which of the approximately 6,500 parishes of the Latin rite your ancestors belonged. The book shows churches before the first partition in 1772. A second useful map book is *Roman Catholic Parishes in the Polish People's Republic in 1984* by Lidia Mullerowa. This book helps in locating parishes in modern Poland. It shows the diocese and deanery to which each parish belongs. Therefore, the book can be useful to determine the correct Polish parish or archive to write for information. There are 58 black and white maps, an 88-page index of towns and villages shown on the maps, and a guide to the names of Polish parishes.

Jewish researchers will benefit from *Discovering Your Jewish Ancestors* by Barbara Krasner-Khait. This book will give you a step-by-step blueprint to help and guide you. An extensive reference to Internet sites that contain material of use to Jewish genealogists is included. A perennial reference book is *Jewish Roots in Poland: Pages from the Past and Archival Inventories* by Miriam Weiner. It is a good read for all Polonia.

I needed to get up to speed on research in Galicia for my paternal line and two books really helped. The first was Gerald A. Ortell's *Polish Parish Records of the Roman Catholic Church: Their Use and Understanding in Genealogical Research*. Based on his own successful research, his book outlines the steps and nuances of records in southern Poland. The second book was the *Genealogical Gazetteer of Galicia* by Brian J. Lenius. He covers the pre-World War I Austrian Crownland of Galizien (Galicia). It includes over 14,000 place names with twelve maps and is based on 1896-1914 information. An easy-to-use gazetteer, it cross references village names from German to Polish, Polish to Ukrainian, etc. In it you will find all the administrative and judicial districts identified and where to locate land ownership (cadastral) maps. The religious districts for Evangelical, Greek Orthodox, Jewish, Mennonite, and Roman Catholic faiths are listed for each village, town, city, and state.

How do I read the records?

You found your ancestors' records and now you need to know what they mean. A research library is not complete without *In their Words: A Genealogist's Translation Guide to Polish, German, Latin, and Russian Documents* by Jonathan D. Shea and William F. Hoffman. Almost any type of document you have, and many you wish to find, are illustrated in Shea and Hoffman's guide to Polish documents (volume I) and Russian documents (volume II). The Polish volume also includes key phrases found in letters from Polish Archives. Judith Frazin's *A Translation Guide to 19th-Century Polish-Language Civil-Registration Documents* should not be overlooked. It contains a list of Hebrew names most often found in Polish records. A useful translation guide for German documents from Prussia and Posen is Edna M. Bentz's *If I Can, You Can Decipher Germanic Records*. This book covers the Gothic alphabet and shows variations of handwritten script for each letter. Do not just look at the handwritten script examples of common genealogical words. In order to learn how to decipher the script, make photocopies of the pages and trace the words, symbols, and common abbreviations found in Germanic records.

To give credibility to your research you must cite your sources. Web sites offer generic citations and genealogy software has templates to help create a source list. Here is a citation from the U.S. census collection on Generations Network (***www.ancestry.com***). Source Citation (It does not include the family name):

- Year: 1900; Census Place: Detroit Ward 14, Wayne, Michigan; Roll: T623 752; Page: 3B; Enumeration District: 156

The same record from HeritageQuest (online via your local FHC or public library):

- JEPKO, THOMAS (1900 U.S. census), MICHIGAN , WAYNE, 14-WD DETROIT, Age: 52, Male, Race: WHITE, Born: AUST, Series: T623 Roll: 752 Page: 247.

As I explored the possibility of becoming a professional genealogist, I attended a weeklong seminar held in Salt Lake City, Utah. We were required to submit a report according to professional standards that focused on a specific research problem. I selected my grandmother, Agata Zdziebko (see page 10). That is how I became acquainted with *Evidence! Citation & Analysis For The Family Historian* by Elizabeth Shown Mills. She writes that research, evidence, citation, and analysis are inseparable:

> *Evidence is the vehicle that moves our research from curiosity to reality.*
> *Citation and analysis are the twin highways that get us there, smoothly and safely.*
> *Successful research—research that yields correct information with a minimum of*
> *wasted time and funds—depends upon a sound analysis of evidence.*

Mills provides a reliable standard for both the correct form of source citation and the sound analysis of evidence. Her newest edition covers electronic formats, including emails, online databases, and message boards. Here are citations from my report using Mills' format:

- Death Certificate: Andrew Zdziebko (Jepko) Henry, death certificate no. 147383 (1931), Michigan Department of Public Heath, Lansing.
- Sacramental Records: Marriage: Vol. 1, Marriage Register, Nov. 1882-July 1909: entry 1, page 30, St. Casimir Catholic Church, Detroit, Michigan.
- Personal letter: From Verna Bivins (Livonia, MI) to Ceil Wendt Jensen 5/22/1977 held in 1999 by Jensen (10399 Anystreet, Hometown, MI 48312). Verna Bivins was the daughter-in-law of Zofia Zdziebko.

What should I look for in the U.S. Census?

While the census was never designed with genealogists in mind, the information they provide give us a useful profile of our families. There were standard questions asked during each enumeration: address; name; relationship to family head; sex; race; age; marital status. Begin with the 1930 census and work your way back. Review the census taker guidelines and questions before starting a new census and pay special attention to the questions about the language spoken and place of birth. The FHC has blank census forms online (see page 13).

1940 Census

The 1940 census, official date April 1, will be released in 2012 and will indicate participation in the Works Progress Administration (WPA) or the Civilian Conservation Corps (CCC). The enrollment papers for these 1930s government relief programs are available via the National Archives and Records Administration's (NARA) National Personnel Records Center in St. Louis. In the 1940 census, residents were asked where they resided in 1935. Because boundary changes were occurring during this period in Europe, enumerators were instructed to record the birthplace as it was situated on January 1, 1937. This impacted Austria and Poland and caused some confusion. If they could not determine with certainty the country in which the person's birthplace was located, they entered the name of the province, state, or city.

1930 Census

The 1930 census official date was April 2, 1930. Useful data includes the name of the country of birth, language spoken in the home before coming to the United States, and birthplace of parents. If the parents' birthplace was different, it would denote migration in Europe. Personal data included school attendance, literacy in any language, ability to speak English, and age at first marriage.

1920 Census

The official date for the census was January 1, 1920. Both the year of immigration and the year of naturalization were recorded. The birthplace of the resident and parents was given. Their mother tongue and their ability to speak English were assessed. Since Poland was back on the map after 123 years, the enumerator had to keep in mind the pre-World War I boundaries. They were to specify the pre-World War I city or town of birth or province, such as German or Russian Poland or Galicia, i.e. Austrian Poland.

1910 Census

The official date was April 1, 1910. The length of the present marriage was recorded and women were asked the number of children born and the number living. When applicable, the year of immigration was recorded. This date might differ from other censuses. Genealogists have more faith in data recorded closest to the occurrence of the event.

RESEARCH LOG

Ancestor's Name: Agatha Zdziebko Agata Zdziebko Wendt

Locality: Records in the state of Michigan

Objectives: Find her nuclear family in Detroit, MI Locate her ancestral village in Galicia

Date of Search	Location / Call Number	Description of Source (author, title, year, pages)	Comments (Purpose of search, results, years and names searched)	Document Number
8 April 1977	Marriage Record Michigan Frank J. Wendt & Agatha Zdziebko	State of Michigan 31 Dec 1899	Birthplace: Russia, Father: John Zdziebko Maiden name of Mother: Unknown	
12 April 1977	Death Certificate #3278 Agatha Zdziebko Wendt	State of Michigan 27 June1908	Search for parents names and village Agatha birthplace: Austria, Father: Czepko, Austria, Mother: unknown	3278
3 May 1977	Death Certificate # 373227 Mary Zdziebko Wendt	State of Michigan 5 December 1947	Search for parents names and village Mary birthplace: Poland, Father: Joseph Zdziebko Mother: Elizabeth	373227
27 May 1977	Baptismal Certificate Frank J. Wendt	17 December 1904 St. Francis D'Assisi Church Detroit, MI	Child of Frank Wendt :330 Buchanan Agatha Zdziebko: Austria	
27 May 1977	Marriage License Michigan Frank J. Wendt & Mary Zdziebko	20 October 1908 St. Francis D'Assisi Detroit, MI	Mary: birthplace: Austria Father: Joseph, Mother: Katherine both mothers are entered as Katherine (error)	64217
June, 1977	Burton Collection Detroit Public Library Det. MI	Detroit City Directory 1899-1923 Extraction of Zdziebko/Jepko	Identified Zdziebko/Jepko residents of Rich St., Kopernick, Buchanan, Otis, Ingersol	
October, 1999	Felician Sisters Archives Livonia, Michigan	Information on the stay of Sylvia (Sophie) Zdziebko in the Guardian Angels Orphanage	Sophie Zdziebko b. May, 1885 birth: Detroit, MI Stay: Oct. 4, 1898 to June 19, 1909 Father: no name listed, Mother: Mary	
1999	Michigan Archives	Naturalization Papers Thomas Jepko	March 15, 1895 Book 10, p. 8165 (p. 354 Index)	
July, 1999	Vol. 84, E.D. 156, Sheet 3 Line 71 Film roll 258	1900 U.S. Federal Census	Thomas Jepko immigrated 1879 with wife Agata and sons John and Frank	
July, 1999	Henry C Jepko	1900 U.S. Federal Census	Henry immigrated in 1878	
July, 1999	Frank Wendt and wife Agatha Zdziebko	1900 U.S. Federal Census	Agatha immigrated 1889	
July, 1999	Frank Wendt and wife Mary Zdziebko	1910 U.S. Federal Census	Mary immigrated 1890	
July, 1999	Thomas Jepko and wife Agatha	1910 U.S. Federal Census	Thomas immigrated 1880	
July, 1999	Wayne Co. MI	World War I registration	No listing of Jepko, Zdziebko	
July, 1999	No listing of Zdziebko, Jepko	1880 Michigan Census Index		

RESEARCH LOG

Ancestor's Name:

Objectives:

Locality:

Date of Search	Location / Call Number	Description of Source (author, title, year, pages)	Comments (Purpose of search, results, years and names searched)	Document Number

Twelfth Census of the United States. This was the only U.S. census to record Łucja and Michal Adamski (line 44-45). Their date of immigration is listed as their son's 1893 date. They actually arrived May 25, 1900, a week before the census's official starting date of June 1. Łucja's first name is recorded phonetically, as Ocea (woosia).

1900 Census

June 1, 1900 was the official date of this census. At this point Poland was not a country. Thus, in cases where a person spoke Polish, the enumerator was required to ask whether their birthplace was what was then known as German Poland, Austrian Poland, or Russian Poland; the answer was accordingly recorded as Poland (Ger.), Poland (Aust.), or Poland (Russ.). If a foreign-born resident had not yet taken steps toward becoming an American citizen, directions were to write "Al" (for alien). Those who had declared their intention to become an American citizen and had taken out "first" papers were noted with "Pa" (for papers). Those who had become a full citizen by taking out "second" or final papers of naturalization were identified with "Na" (for naturalization). The 1900 census is a favorite of genealogists today because it asked for a resident's month and year of birth as well as age at last birthday.

1890 Census

Most of these census schedules were destroyed by a fire in 1921. Some online sites substitute 1890s-era city directories for this census.

1880 Census

The official date was June 1, 1880 and it was a simple census compared to the ones that followed. There were no questions about language, immigration, or citizenship. Only the place of birth of the resident and their parents gives an indication of foreign birth. The enumerator was instructed to be specific and enter the state as Prussia, instead of the country as Germany. We find entries such as Prussia-Poland, Galicia-Austria, and Silesia-Germany.

1900 United States Federal Census

State: _____
County: _____
City, township: _____

Call Number/URL: _____

Enumeration District: _____
Sheet Number: _____
Enumeration Date: _____

Location			Name	Relation	Personal Description										Nativity		

Location — In Cities: Street; House number. Number of dwelling house in the order of visitation (1). Number of family, in the order of visitation (2). Line number.

Name (3) — of each person whose place of abode on June 1, 1900, was in this family. Enter surname first, then the given name and middle initial, if any. Include every person living on June 1, 1900. Omit children born since June 1, 1900.

Relation (4) — Relationship of each person to the head of the family.

Personal Description — Color or Race (5); Sex (6); Date of Birth: Month, Year (7); Age at last birthday (8); Whether single, married, widowed, or divorced (9); Number of years of present marriage (10); Mother of how many children (11); Number of these children living (12).

Nativity — Place of birth of each person and parents of each person enumerated. If born in United States, give state or territory. If foreign birth, give the country. Place of birth of this person (13); Place of birth of Father of this person (14); Place of birth of Mother of this person (15).

Citizenship — Year of immigration to the U.S. (16); Number of years in the U.S. (17); Naturalization (18).

Occupation, Trade, or Profession of each person TEN YEARS of age and over — Occupation (19); Months not employed (20).

Education — Attended school (in months) (21); Can read (22); Can write (23); Can speak English (24).

Ownership of Home — Owned or Rented (25); Owned free or mortgaged (26); Farm or house (27); Number of farm schedule (28).

NOTES:

1900 Census.
Find blank census forms online under FHL's Research Guidance - Articles.
www.familysearch.org

What genealogy information is in a City Directory?

It is natural to study city directories after census research. City directories can fill in the years between each decimal census. While directories have been published in the U.S. since the 1700s, the books printed for the year 1890 are of high value for Pol-Am researchers. They can serve as a substitute for the 1890 U.S. census information destroyed by a fire in 1921—a great loss for researchers whose ancestors were recent immigrants.

The 1890 book for your ancestors' town or city answers a few of the questions asked in the 11th U.S. census. The census extended its scope to cover its subjects in greater detail. The city directory will not answer the census questions about ethnicity; nor will it often list marital status or relationship to the head of the household. However, it does give city, house number, and street names; and answers the questions of occupation and home ownership.

Make use of the front and back matter of the directory. Become familiar with the abbreviations presented in the front matter and used throughout the book. Some of the abbreviations are universal for all books, such as "av" for avenue; "c", corner; "RR", railroad; "wid", widow. But books will have very specific abbreviations for the regions, such as in the Philadelphia, Pennsylvania book. Some abbreviations for its towns and villages are: Bln, Bustleton; C Hill, Chestnut Hill; Rox, Roxborough; Schyl, Schuylkill. Back matter includes households by street and in numeric order. It is a great way to see who was in the neighborhood. City directories can also offer insight into the life and times if you read the ads that are showcased on banners throughout the book.

After extracting your family in the 1890 city directory, expand your use of those same directories. The chart provided on page 17 will help you organize the information that may detail your knowledge of your ancestors' occupations, residences, and neighbors.

Quite often, you will find that your ancestor married the girl or boy next door. For this reason it is very useful to chart the whole neighborhood. The neighbors from the 1900 city directory may become aunts and uncles in the 1910 directory. A sample map on page 19 was created from the back matter listing by street address.

City directories are available in a range of formats. There are the actual directories in book form sitting on the library shelf; but a book printed in 1900 is apt to leave a lot of "confetti" on the table. Some libraries wisely offer bound photocopies of the original for patrons. Other formats include microfilm and microfiche, as well as digital copies online offered by Ancestry and HeritageQuest. Many state and local public libraries have these directories on their Web site. If you are purchasing directories on CD, check to see if the directory is a digital scan or an extraction. Each and every extraction opens a chance for more errors.

Tracking the Zdziebko family in a number of city directories for different years resulted in the following spelling variations of the name:

1886 Zavziepko	1910 Zdziepko	1913 Zdziezko	1920 Zdierko
1920 Jepko	1921 Zdziebo	1938 Zdyzebko	

Instead of getting irked that the name has been slaughtered, jot down the variations to use in search engines when the true spelling does not return results. Do not be surprised to find your surname spelled in a variety of ways!

Some researchers track down original ownership of the family home long after it has been sold. The example to the right documents changes in a neighborhood known as Swedetown in Calumet, Houghton County, Michigan. It presents the earlier Polish residences of Szatkowski and Zawada.

One last important note about using city directories is that for a range of reasons, including safety and mail delivery, many cities have renumbered houses and have changed street names. Stephen P. Morse, PhD, Joel D. Weintraub, PhD, and David R. Kehs, PhD, have collected links to online directories for city Web sites with street name changes. They have generated tables for other cities where data was in print form. On Steve Morse's One-Step Web site, he can link you to his Web page entitled *Obtaining Street Name Changes in One Step*. Many American cities are detailed including Chicago, whose street numbering was described as chaotic prior to 1909. One of the problems was that the number on one street did not correspond to the same location on a parallel street. ***www.stevemorse.org***

> **3030 Bridge St.**
>
> Szatkowski, John 1891
>
> Szatkowski, John & Wikerich, Victoria......1897
>
> Szatkowski, John & Louise...........................1899
>
> Szatkowski, John & Louise, Wikerich, Victoria..1908
>
> Zawada, Frank..1910
>
> Zawada, Frank & Victoria............................1916
>
> Aho, Eino..1930
>
> No longer standing.......................................1940

Polish residence supplanted by the Finns. This data is from Swedetown, for the New Millennium (Medved).

Grouped under Chicago, Illinois are links for: *RootsWeb utility-street index; Link to Polish Genealogical Society list; Link to 1909 pdf file of renumbering changes; Link to 1928/1929 pdf file of Polk City Directory; Link to Chicago Museum pdf files (1909, 1911, and 1948).* The One-Step site has additional tools for census work. Ahead of the game, they already have tools for the highly anticipated release of the 1940 U.S. Federal Census on April 2, 2012.

City, State; Detroit, Michigan		Burton Historical Collection, Detroit, July, 1977		
Surname	**Spelling**	**Given Name**	**Occupation**	**Address**
1889				
ADAMSKI	Adamsky	Michael	lab.	h. 334 Concord Ave.
PRZYTULSKI	-	-	-	-
WENDT	Wendt	Frank	teamster	bds. 141 Eliot
WOJTKOWIAK	-	-	-	-
ZDZIEBKO	-	-	-	-
1890				
ADAMSKI	Adamsky	Michael	molder	h. 249 Pierce
PRZYTULSKI	-	-	-	-
WENDT	Wendt	Frank	-	gone to Chicago
WOJTKOWIAK	Wojtkowiak	Joseph	lab.	h. 380 22nd St.
ZDZIEBKO	-	-	-	-
1891				
ADAMSKI	Adamski	Joseph	carp.	h. 608 23rd St.
WENDT	-	-	-	-
WOJTKOWIAK	Wojtkowiak	Joseph	lab.	380 22nd St.
ZDZIEBKO	Zdziebko	Andrew	mach. hd.	bds. 169 Rich St.
		Thomas	lab.	h. 169 Rich St.
1892				
ADAMSKI	-	-	-	-
PRZYTULSKI	-	-	-	-
WENDT	-	-	-	-
WOJTKOWIAK	Wojtkowiak	Joseph	lab.	380 22nd St.
ZDZIEBKO	-	-	-	-
1893				
ADAMSKI	Adamski	Anton	lab.	658 Farnsworth
	Adamski	Mathais	molder	h. 665 Forest
	Adamski	Michael	molder	419 Illinois
PRZYTULSKI	-	-	-	-
WENDT	Wendt	Frank	lab.	bds. 581 Hancock
WOJTKOWIAK	Wojtkowiak	Joseph	lab.	380 22nd St.
	Wojtkowiak	Peter	lab.	90 26th St.
ZDZIEBKO	Zdziebko	Andrew	lab.	bds.169 Rich
		Frank	lab.	bds.169 Rich
		Henry	mach.	bds.169 Rich
		John	lab.	bds.169 Rich
		Thomas	lab.	h. 169 Rich

*Extraction of data for surnames: Adamski, Przytulski, Wendt,
Wojtkowiak, and Zdziebko from Detroit city directories 1889-1893.*

City, State		Research Facility		
Surname	Spelling	Given Name	Occupation	Address
Year				

Use this chart to organize the family data found in city directories.

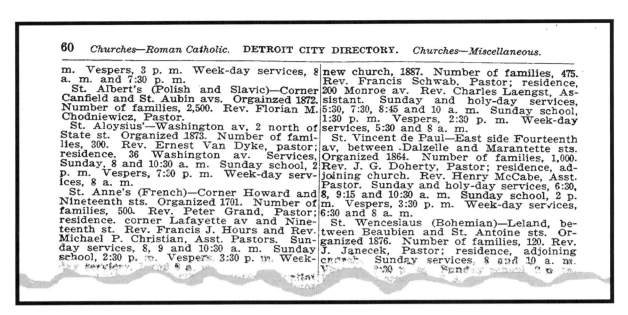

60   *Churches—Roman Catholic.*   DETROIT CITY DIRECTORY.   *Churches—Miscellaneous.*

m. Vespers, 3 p. m. Week-day services, 8 a. m. and 7:30 p. m.

St. Albert's (Polish and Slavic)—Corner Canfield and St. Aubin avs. Organized 1872. Number of families, 2,500. Rev. Florian M. Chodniewicz, Pastor.

St. Aloysius'—Washington av, 2 north of State st. Organized 1873. Number of families, 300. Rev. Ernest Van Dyke, pastor; residence. 36 Washington av. Services, Sunday, 8 and 10:30 a. m. Sunday school, 2 p. m. Vespers, 7:30 p. m. Week-day services, 8 a. m.

St. Anne's (French)—Corner Howard and Nineteenth sts. Organized 1701. Number of families, 500. Rev. Peter Grand, Pastor; residence. corner Lafayette av and Nineteenth st. Rev. Francis J. Hours and Rev. Michael P. Christian, Asst. Pastors. Sunday services, 8, 9 and 10:30 a. m. Sunday school, 2:30 p. m. Vespers 3:30 p. m. Week-

new church, 1887. Number of families, 475. Rev. Francis Schwab. Pastor; residence, 200 Monroe av. Rev. Charles Laengst, Assistant. Sunday and holy-day services, 5:30, 7:30, 8:45 and 10 a. m. Sunday school, 1:30 p. m. Vespers, 2:30 p. m. Week-day services, 5:30 and 8 a. m.

St. Vincent de Paul—East side Fourteenth av, between Dalzelle and Marantette sts. Organized 1864. Number of families, 1,000. Rev. J. G. Doherty, Pastor; residence, adjoining church. Rev. Henry McCabe, Asst. Pastor. Sunday and holy-day services, 6:30, 8, 9:15 and 10:30 a. m. Sunday school, 2 p. m. Vespers, 3:30 p. m. Week-day services, 6:30 and 8 a. m.

St. Wenceslaus (Bohemian)—Leland, between Beaubien and St. Antoine sts. Organized 1876. Number of families, 120. Rev. J. Janecek, Pastor; residence, adjoining church. Sunday services, 8 and 10 a. m.

Front Matter, showing Churches-Miscellaneous including St. Albertus erroneously listed as St. Albert's. Detroit City Directory. Detroit: R.L. Polk & Co., 1894.

By using the city directory data and the Sanborn fire insurance maps, a personalized map of your ancestor's neighborhood can be generated. The Sanborn Digital Map collection can be found online via subscribing public libraries and universities.

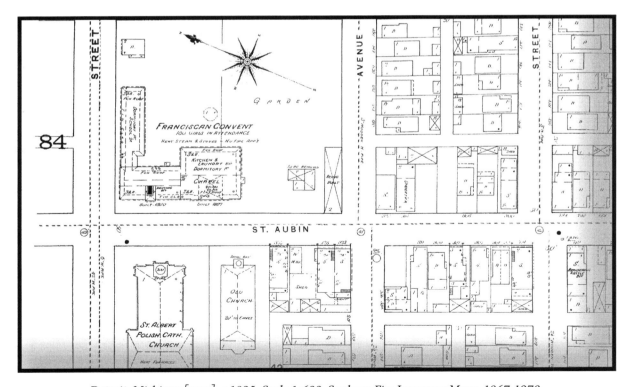

Detroit, Michigan [map], c.1895. Scale 1:600. Sanborn Fire Insurance Maps, 1867-1970.

Alexandrine av (576) intersects.
n e cor Campbell School
771 Kolch Josephine, saloon
" Feike Conrad
781 Maday A, real estate
782 Drager C F, shoes
783 Rutkewicz Joseph
784 Friedberg Samuel
" Krahn Martha, millinry
789 Kreft August, meats
790 Brzozowski A, paints
Superior st (436) intersects.
794 Welsand John, shoes
797 Ostrowski M J, saloon
" Bialk John
799 Lemke John
800 Bierowski Joseph, saln
" Bolda Joseph
801 Sikora Joseph
" Wittstock Anton
802 Grinke Martin
805 Piotrowski F, shoes
" Dyament S, barber
806 Mroch August
807 Morowski Bros, bakers
" Sikora Anton, contr
809 Treppa Martin
" Koschitzkowski C
811-815 Lemke A, hardware
" Treinis Henrietta
812 Chilinski Wm, clothing
816 Kulwicki Bros, undtkrst
820 Kroll Adolph, pictures

820 Stryzewski Julius F, ci-
gar mnfr
Willis av (576) intersects.
823-825 Lemke A, grocer
833 Lemke V T, dry goods
w s Chodniewicz Rev F M
s w cor St Adelbertus Ch
s e cor St Francis' Convent
Canfield av (531) intersects.
n w cor St Albert's Polish
School
860 Kaminecki Martin, saln
862 Kott Joseph
864 Wobrach M, dry goods
866 Sochalski J, blacksmith
868 Nikelewski P, furn mfr
869-871 Hope Mark F, flour
870 Schultz John
875 Selkie August, clothing
877-879 Gohr Anthony, grocr
878 Povinski Jacob
" Milosch Joseph
880 Funke Joseph
884 Jozefowicz Constance
" Szjnizewski Andrew
886 Mroczkowski Kajetan
" Ostrowski Bernard J
892 Koppenhagen Anton
" Maciejewski Anton
894 Dettloff Joseph
" Owczarek Jacob
" Hirt John
896 Sandow Thomas
Albert pl (56) ends.

Garfield av (580) intersects.
912 Busch August
" Grzibowski L, meats
n w cor Niedziela Polish
Weekly
w s St Mary's Seminary
916 Krausmann A, dairy
918 Herberger Catherine M
Forest av (596) intersects.
946 Brichel Joseph, saloon
947 Olejniczak F, shoes
" Dysarz August
" Harms Ernest
" Resner August
952 Trinskewicz A, grocer
" Stanka Frank
954 Piper Bernhard
" Dettloff Augusta
960 Plumb Susan
962 Bora Anton
" Brosowski Frank
966 Piontke August
968 Schwartz Maximilian
" Schwartz Adam
970 Bromberak Stanislaus

Image at left: Back Matter p. 1721 (amended), Detroit City Directory. Detroit: R.L. Polk & Co., 1894.

Image at left: Map made by author showing the cross streets, residences, and businesses in the St. Albertus neighborhood.

Finding birth records

Whether you are researching in U.S. or Polish records, you will want to use the rule of thumb of looking for a birth every two years. If there is an interruption in the births, the couple may have been separated by employment or the immigration process. The chart below was created using Mike Smith's *Family Estimator*. It is now offline; but generated the chart based on the following parameters. It took a single date and event for one person and estimated and built a whole family group sheet for them. It was designed from the information of over 100,000 computerized genealogical records from Western Europe and North America, stored in the LDS database. The logic was that people marry between the ages of 18-24, the first child will come one year later, and so forth. The reasoning carries that each person will live an average of X years depending on when they were born and that women will live longer than men. It also suggested the date of death. It offered a point in time to start looking, plus or minus eight years. Improvements in medicine and life spans were taken into account; but the estimator could not accommodate for wars, plagues, illegitimate children, early births, accidental deaths, or divorces.

Husband Birth Abt 1822		Family ZDZIEBKO		Husband Death Abt 1888
Wife Birth: Abt 1824		Marriage: Abt 1846		Wife Death: Abt 1890
Child 1	B: Abt 1847	M: Abt 1870	D: Abt 1913	Age 8: Abt 1855
Child 2	B: Abt 1848	M: Abt 1871	D: Abt 1914	Age 8: Abt 1856
Child 3	B: Abt 1850	M: Abt 1873	D: Abt 1916	Age 8: Abt 1858
Child 4	B: Abt 1852	M: Abt 1875	D: Abt 1918	Age 8: Abt 1860
Child 5	B: Abt 1854	M: Abt 1877	D: Abt 1920	Age 8: Abt 1862
Child 6	B: Abt 1856	M: Abt 1879	D: Abt 1922	Age 8: Abt 1864
Child 7	B: Abt 1858	M: Abt 1881	D: Abt 1924	Age 8: Abt 1866
Child 8	B: Abt 1860	M: Abt 1883	D: Abt 1926	Age 8: Abt 1868

Suggested births, marriage, and death dates for the Zdziebko family 1822-1890.

A four-generation maternal line portrait of (l to r) Mariana, Cecilia, Jacquelyn, and Genevieve. c. 1944.

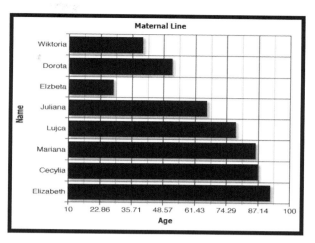

Longevity of a maternal line beginning in 1725 in Poznań.

Longevity is the length of a person's life or life expectancy. Significant factors that contribute to an individual's longevity include gender, genetics, access to health care, hygiene, and war. Pedigree charts are intriguing not only for family history; but, also, for family health. The chart illustrated above shows a maternal line whose longevity far exceeded the life expectancy for their eras. Only one woman died early as a result of tuberculosis.

Pictured above are four women who carry the H haplogroup mtDNA, a genetic marker passed down by mother to her children. During an informal discussion with mtDNA expert, Dr. Bryan Sykes, author of *The Seven Daughters of Eve*, he stated that the H haplogroup is the standard in Europe because these women were healthy and lived long enough to procreate. Former U.S. Surgeon General Carmona created the *Family History Initiative*, launched to encourage all American families to learn more about their family health history.

Common diseases such as heart disease, cancer, and diabetes can run in families. Tracing the illnesses suffered by your parents, grandparents, and other blood relatives can help your doctor predict the disorders for which you may be at risk and take action to keep you and your family healthy. Use *My Family Health Portrait* online or download the ready-to-print version. It helps organize your family history information. The site can be accessed via the Internet. ***www.familyhistory.hhs.gov***

Graphical representation of your family's health disorders that may move from one generation to the next can be created. This is a powerful tool for predicting any illnesses for which you should be checked. There is a downloadable *My Family Health Portrait* software accessible online. ***www.hhs.gov/familyhistory/downloads/portraitEng.pdf***

How do I find my parents' birth certificates?

Individual states began to collect data for birth, marriages, and deaths in the late 1890s. The chart on page 30 summarizes the years Pol-Am states began their collections. Before that time, records were registered on the local level. This may mean looking at the parish registry where the baptism was recorded.

Baptisms usually took place a day or two after a child's birth. Recorded in Latin, the priest entered the number of the birth in the parish, date of birth, date of baptism, legitimacy, and names of the parents and godparents. Traditionally, godparents were family members and by accepting the role of godparent, they accepted responsibility of raising the child as a Catholic if the parents died.

For births at home, the midwife or doctor would file the birth certificate. If a certificate was not available, the adult could go to probate court and petition for a delayed birth certificate.

1883 Roman Catholic Baptismal record.
Latin headers read: name of infant and residence, date of birth (day, month, year), date of baptism (day, month, year), names of parents, and names of godparents.

Check with your probate court or department of health for delayed birth certificates. These can be interesting documents since family members or a neighbor had to vouch for the birth. Some small U.S. towns published *Hospital Notes* providing birth announcements. Research that county's library for availability of archived newspapers.

The terrorist attacks on September 11, 2001 caused new restrictions for obtaining copies of birth certificates. You will need to check with the local or state department of health for their current requirements. Many online Web sites have extractions or indexes for births. Rootsweb, Ancestry, and your local state ahrchives are the best places to start. Some sites allow online order submissions. ***www.vitalchek.com***

It is a good idea to collect information on all siblings when extracting information from state or parochial records. The form on page 23 helps document your findings. The comments column can record godparents' notes. Church scribes have often been known to write in the marriage or death of a parishioner on their baptismal records. Also, it is not unusual to find notations of a surname change and the date the court approved it.

Birth / Christening Register Extraction Form

Subject:

Source:

Repository: **Call Number:**

Date	Page/Entry	Child's Name	Father's Name / Mother's Name	Comments

How do you find marriage records for genealogical research?

Your census research will have given you information about marriages that took place. The 1900 census asked for the number of years married, the 1910 census asked for the number of years of present marriage, and the 1930 census asked the age at first marriage. This information and the first child's birthplace help guide you to the appropriate state to look for marriage records. Search for two records: the state-issued license and the religious certificate issued by the minister, priest, or rabbi. Many researchers seek the marriage license not only for the date, but for the names of the bride's and groom's parents. Additional sources of information include marriage banns, engagement and wedding announcements, and sometimes coverage of the wedding in the local newspaper.

Government and Society Records

Vital records (birth, marriage, and death) can be obtained from the county or state Department of Vital Records. You may be able to obtain the information less expensively by using other resources. You can look for indexes and extractions created by local libraries, genealogy societies, historical societies, and archives. For example, the Wisconsin Historical Society has indexes and order forms online. *www.wisconsinhistory.org*

You will need to find out the privacy laws in your state regarding vital records. In the state of New York, for instance, birth records are made available after 75 years; marriage and death indexes after 50 years. Other items to consider are that the requirements for a marriage license and the legal age of marriage varied by state. Dispensations may have been arranged for underage or close relationships. Some "shotgun" marriages took place over the state line where there was no waiting period.

Religious Records

When approaching a parish for records, you need to remember that sacramental records are not public records. It is at the priest's discretion to allow you access. Be ready to make a donation to the church in honor of your ancestors. Do not offer to pay the priest—a subtle but substantial point.

The FHL in Salt Lake City has many religious records on microfilm. You can order films for viewing at a local FHC. Rental charges are minimal and the film is usually available for research at the library for one month. Their catalog is online. *www.familysearch.org*

Select the **Library** tab, followed by the **Library Catalog** tab. Choose **Place Search**. I chose Hammond, Lake County, Indiana, and found they hold microfilm for St. Casimir

Marriage Register Extraction Form

Subject:

Source:

Repository: Call Number:

Date	Page/Entry	Groom / Bride	Groom's Parents / Bride's Parents	Witnesses / Comments

Church from 1891-1993. These microfilmed records originated from the Diocese of Gary, Merrillville County, Indiana. The film I ordered was FHL US/CAN Film 1887905. The notation "Items 1-8" indicates that the information I was seeking would be found within the first eight items on the film. The film also has communions, confirmations, and deaths.

Divorce records are obtained from the county where the divorce took place. A quick search on Ancestry shows databases for Nevada Divorce Index, 1968-2005, Minnesota Divorce Index, 1970-1995, and Texas Divorce Index, 1968-2002. RootsWeb has links to Web sites for most counties in the U.S. as part of their USGenWeb Project. *www.usgenweb.org*

Where do I find death records?

Governmental Records

States started collecting death returns in the late 1800s; but many were not consistent until the early 1900s. Genealogists caution that the information on the death certificate may be faulty. Spouses dealing with grief may not supply accurate information. Note the informant who gave the data about the decedent. Questions asked at the city level may vary from the state document and may have changed over time. It might be smart to look at both. Typically, you will find the name and age of the decedent, place of birth, address, name of spouse, cause of death, funeral director, and the cemetery of burial. Some documents request names of parents and length of time in the county and community.

Sacramental Records

Check the family's home parish for a funeral record. The name, age, cause of death, parents, spouse, and cemetery are among the items that may be entered in the sacramental records.

Funeral Homes

Many turn-of-the-century wakes were held at the family residence after the undertaker (*pogrzebowy*) prepared the body for viewing. The funeral home maintains records of who arranged for the funeral, the place of burial, and sometimes the type of coffin purchased. They should have a copy of the death certificate and are responsible for placing the obituary in the newspaper. Obituaries are valuable sources of genealogical data. Many societies have published them in booklets and online. Local universities and public libraries have newspapers on microfilm and the reference librarian may be willing to do a look up for you. PGSA has online Death Notice Indexes from *Dziennik Chicagoski*, Chicago's Polish daily newspaper. They also published Thomas E. Golembiewski's *The Study of Obituaries as a Source for Genealogical Research*. *www.pgsa.org*

Death & Burial Register Extraction Form

Subject:

Source:

Repository: Call Number:

Date	Page/ Entry	Name	Age	Informant Relationships	Funeral Home / Cemetery

Cemeteries

The sexton or director of the cemetery is required by law to keep records of burials. They also keep records of exhumations and the new cemetery of burial. The cemetery may have additional information if there is a family lot. Ask to see the lot diagram. Cemeteries have been moved due to natural disasters such as flooding and sinking due to underground mines. Some early Pol-Am cemeteries in the U.S. followed the European

Entry in the Otto Schemansky and Sons Monuments order book for the stone for Katherine Maciejewski. It was ordered in 1939 by her son Charles Machesky using the Anglicized version of the surname.

practice of term graves. If the family did not extend the payment of the grave, it was reopened after 25-35 years for a new burial. Remains were removed to an ossuary or tamped down and covered with the new burial. This is still the practice in Poland today. Online genealogists have submitted cemetery data to Interment.net: *www.interment.net* and Find A Grave: *www.findagrave.com*

Monuments and Post-Mortem Photos

It was not uncommon for the immigrant family to have a photo taken of the deceased. These photos were often sent back to the extended family in Poland. If there is a gravestone at the cemetery, it will have the decedent's name and usually the year of birth and death. Some gravestones have portraits as well. If you find the name of the monument maker on the tombstone base, you may be able to obtain records of the sale. A word of caution

though— tombstones can be damaged. Learn how to care for them online. *www.gravestonestudies.org*

Religious Orders

The records of religious orders are a neglected but rich source of genealogical information. When I began researching, I felt I was off track researching auxiliary lines of the family. I had the misconception that while it was respectful to note a family member in a

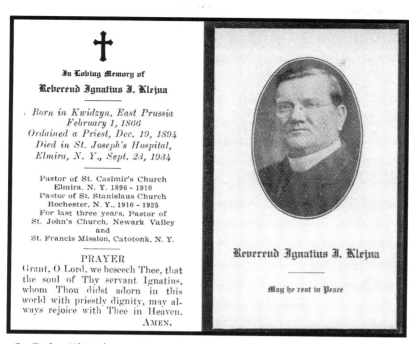

In Loving Memory of
Reberend Ignatius J. Klejna

Born in Kwidzyn, East Prussia
February 1, 1866
Ordained a Priest, Dec. 19, 1894
Died in St. Joseph's Hospital,
Elmira, N. Y., Sept. 23, 1934

Pastor of St. Casimir's Church
Elmira, N. Y. 1896 - 1910
Pastor of St. Stanislaus Church
Rochester, N. Y., 1910 - 1925
For last three years, Pastor of
St. John's Church, Newark Valley
and
St. Francis Mission, Catotonk, N. Y.

PRAYER
Grant, O Lord, we beseech Thee, that
the soul of Thy servant Ignatius,
whom Thou didst adorn in this
world with priestly dignity, may always
rejoice with Thee in Heaven.
AMEN.

Reberend Ignatius J. Klejna

May he rest in Peace

On Father Klejna's very informative memorial funeral card is listed his birth, ordination, and parish affiliations. His birthplace was Kwidzyn, East Prussia. Borders changed after World War II and it is now a village in Poland.

religious order, it was not productive to the research at hand. I was mistaken! If you have a family member who joined a religious order, I encourage you to contact the order's archives and request the Necrology entry. The first two paragraphs of the obituary for my cousin, Brother Humilis, listed valuable genealogical information. If I had requested this information several years earlier, I would have saved a great deal of time and money. Included in the obituary was the name of his birth village, his mother's maiden name, an estimated date of arrival in the U.S., and the number of siblings. A photo of Brother Humilis was published in the article and he bore a handsome resemblance to my grandma.

Funeral Cards

You may have your grandmother's collection of funeral cards stored in her missal. They may contain useful information. Below is a sample translation of one such card written in Polish. PGSA offers a free translation guide online. *www.pgsa.org/PDFs/DzChicObit.pdf*

Błogosławieni są ci, którzy zasnęli w Panu, ponieważ uczynki ich pójdą za nimi. ś.p. Walenty Maciejewski Ur. się 14 Lutego 1854 Umarł 11 Sierpnia 1926 Licząc lat 72	Blessed are those, who died in the lord because their (good) acts will follow them. Saintly memory Walenty Maciejewski born on 14 February 1854 Died 11 August 1926 72 years
Leon A. Mulawa, Pogrzebowy 4410 St. Aubin Ave	Leon A. Mulawa, Undertaker 4410 St. Aubin Ave

Early vital records were kept at the community and county level. The chart below lists the range of civil record keeping in key Polish-American cities and states. Note that the county is given for each city listed. Vital records are now kept at the city, county, and state level and access is governed by law. Check the Internet for their accessibility. The earlier records may be held by historical societies or archives, while more recent records may be held by the local clerk or health department.

Vital Records in Pol-Am States			
State / City (County)	Birth	Marriage	Death
CALIFORNIA	1905	1905	1905
Los Angeles (Los Angeles)	1866	1852	1877
CONNECTICUT	1897	1897	1897
New Britain (Hartford)	1852	1820	1855
ILLINOIS	1916	1962	1916
Chicago (Cook)	1871	1871	1871
INDIANA	1907	1958	1899
East Chicago (Lake)	1882	1837	1882
MARYLAND	1898	1950	1898
Baltimore (Baltimore)	1875	1777	1875
MASSACHUSETTS	1841	1841	1841
Boston (Suffolk)	1870	1870	1870
MICHIGAN	1867	1867	1867
Detroit (Wayne)	1897	1818	1867
MINNESOTA	1900	1958	1908
Minneapolis (Hennepen)	1870	1853	1870
NEW JERSEY	1848	1848	1848
Perth Amboy (Middlesex)	1854	1895	1895
NEW YORK	1880	1880	1880
Buffalo (Erie)	1876	1878	1886
OHIO	1908	1949	1908
Toledo (Lucas)	1867	1835	1868
PENNSYLVANIA	1906	1885	1906
Pittsburgh (Allegheny)	1870	1870	1906
TEXAS	1903	1966	1903
Karnes & Bexar County	1903	1865	1903
WISCONSIN	1907	1907	1907
Milwaukee (Milwaukee)	1835	1836	1872

What information was asked on a Social Security application?

The application for a Social Security Account Number (SSN) asked for the applicant's name, address, birth date, place of birth, and parents' names (living or dead). This is a great source to get the names of the parents, many of whom never came to the United States. Social Security applications were first distributed in late November of 1936; and your immigrant ancestor may have filled one out. The number was issued to track employee taxation.

Social Security Death Index (SSDI)

Web sites offer the SSDI database online; but it does not have all claimants. It has claimants who lived into 1961 and beyond, when the agency began using mainframe computers. You might be able to find an earlier SSN on a Social Security card or employment or death record. Online sites may generate an order form for you to send to the Social Security Administration (SSA). Be alert to the state where the card was issued, the last residence, and where the last SS payment was sent. They may all be different. It can lead to more records in other states.

Form SS-5

Make sure you request the SS-5 form filled out by the applicant. If you do not specify the SS-5 application form, you will receive a record which does not have the parent's names; but does include name changes for married women (this information is not found on the original application). If the SSA cannot find the original application, they will send the abstracted record which has less information. The SSA has copies of pre-1961 applications. If you request a search without the Social Security number, the fee is $29.00; with the number, it is $27.00.

This Social Security application was filled out by Walter Adamski on March 4, 1943. While he resided in Detroit, it documents his birth in Red Jacket, a mining village in the township of Calumet in the Upper Peninsula of Michigan.

FAMILY GROUP: _____			FAMILY NUMBER:

HUSBAND'S NAME:

Compiled by:	Event	Date	Place or Name
	Birth		
	Baptism		
	Marriage		
	Death		
	Burial		
	Occupation or Profession		
	Father's Name		
	Mother's Name		
	Other Spouses		
	Notes		

WIFE'S NAME:

Sources:	Event	Date	Place or Name
	Birth		
	Baptism		
	Death		
	Burial		
	Occupation or Profession		
	Father's Name		
	Mother's Name		
	Other Spouses		
	Notes		

MF	Name of Child &Spouse	Event	Date	Place
1		Birth		
		Marriage		
		Death		
		Burial		
2		Birth		
		Marriage		
		Death		
		Burial		
3		Birth		
		Marriage		
		Death		
		Burial		
4		Birth		
		Marriage		
		Death		
		Burial		
5		Birth		
		Marriage		
		Death		
		Burial		
6		Birth		
		Marriage		
		Death		
		Burial		

The Family Group Sheet is an easy form to use when you are extracting data or want to share research.

Chapter 3:
U.S. Military Records

The period of 1880-1920 was the height of Polish immigration to the United States. The United States required every young man between the ages of 18 and 45 to register for the World War I draft regardless of their citizenship. The World War I draft registration required eligible foreign born men to provide the name of their birth village. If you are tracing a female ancestor, make sure to check this data for male members of the family.

World War I draft registration cards can be accessed via FHL, Ancestry, or the NARA in Atlanta, Georgia. The draft included 24 million men born between 1873 and 1900 and took place in three stages. The first draft on June 5, 1917 registered men (ages 21-31) born between June 6, 1886 and June 5, 1896. The men reported to their draft board and answered 12 questions. Of high interest to the Pol-Am researcher are the questions asked in item 4 regarding naturalization: Are you (1) a natural-born citizen; (2) a naturalized citizen; (3) an alien; or (4) have you declared your intention? Item 5 asked: Where were you born? (Town, state, nation). Item 6 requested: If not a citizen, of what country are you a citizen or subject? The question regarding disability may reveal a missing finger cut off to avoid the draft in

Draft registration card of Anthony Przytulski. Born in 1890, he was registered during the first draft, June 5, 1917. His birthplace, Kuczbork, is spelled phonetically: Cutsburg.

Poland. The second draft, held on June 5, 1918, registered men who had turned 21 and were born between June 6, 1896 and June 5, 1897. The registration question about birth had been expanded and asked for the father's birthplace (city or town, state or province, and nation). Draftees were asked about citizenship and if they were an alien; and if so, which nation they were a subject. Other useful genealogical information includes: name of employer, place of employment, and name and complete address of their nearest relative.

A third draft, held on September 12, 1918 required all men ages 18-21 and 31-45 to register if they had not already done so. The itemized questions included: Are you (10) native born, (11) naturalized, (12) a citizen by father's naturalization? If they were an alien, they specified if they were a declarant or non-declarant. Question (15) asked: If not a citizen of the U.S., of what nation are you a citizen or subject?

Surname Study

Since brothers, cousins, and neighbors all registered for the draft, it provides a database for a surname study. I began a project to see if I could determine my grandmother's village using her relatives' information. Since there are about 400 people using the name in Poland today, but far fewer in Detroit in 1917, I searched for the Zdziebko draft cards. I added Ambrozy—a surname mentioned as the next of kin. Some family members had already anglicized their name, so they had to be accounted for as well. My immediate family reported that they were naturalized under their father's 1900 petition so they did not enter a Polish location.

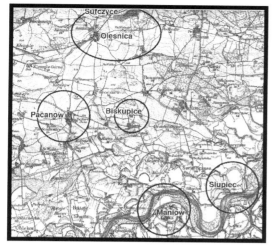

Zdziebko Birth Villages

Using the data from draft cards, I plotted locations on a 1910 map; and the villages clustered along the border of Russian Poland and Galicia. Additional searching proved this was indeed the area from which my Zdziebko's hailed. Great-grandfather Jan Zdziebko was born in 1837 in Maniów; his father, Wojciech, in Pacanów; and John came from Biskupice.

See the Ambrozy/Zdziebko data that follows:

Name	Birth Date	Birthplace	Nearest Relative
John Zdziebko	9 June 1888	Biskupice, Russian Poland	Wife & Child
Charles Zdziebko	4 September 1881	Russian Poland	sister, Rose Ambrozy
Steve Ambrozy	12 April 1895	Olesnica, Russian Poland	wife, Rose Ambrozy

What was the Blue Army (a.k.a. Haller's Army)?

The Blue Army *(Błękitna Armia)* and Haller's Army *(Armia Hallera)* are interchangeable informal names given to the Polish Army units formed in France (Armia Polska we Francyi) during the later stages of World War I. The nicknames come from the soldiers' French blue uniforms and the name of the army's commander, General Józef Haller de Hallenburg. An estimated 20,000 Polish descendants, Christians and Jews alike, answered the call to fight for freedom and the opportunity to regain Poland's independence during World War I.

Recruitment took place as early as October, 1917 in cities with large Polish populations including Boston, Buffalo, Chicago, Detroit, and Wilkes-Barre, Pennsylvania. The recruitment applications were microfilmed by the PGSA. Their online database can be searched and, for a small fee, copies of the records can be ordered. *www.pgsa.org/haller.php* The Ambrozy search results are illustrated below:

Name	Location	Volume	Page	Form
Ambrozy, Antoni	Detroit, MI		ABC	L
Ambrozy, Jan	Minneapolis, MN		ABC	L
Ambrozy, Jan	Chicago, IL		ABC	L
Ambrozy, Stanislaw	Detroit, MI	253	74	C

ARMIA POLSKA WE FRANCYI

AKT ZGŁOSZENIA DO ARMII POLSKIEJ WE FRANCYI.

*Additional research on the Ambrozy line identified
Stanislaw as an applicant for the Armia Polska we Francyi.*

When you are requesting your ancestors' files, you need to know: Form A is an intention to volunteer and records the birthplace and closest relative in the U.S. and Poland; Form B is a medical examination; and Form C is the final commitment paper and contains the most significant genealogical information.

Seven ships carrying returning Haller's Army soldiers departing from Danzig have been identified: *SS Antigone* (April 18, 1920), *SS Latvia* (August 17, 1922), *SS Mercury* (June 28, 1920), *SS Pocahontas* (April 21, 1920 and June 16, 1920), *SS President Grant* (February 16, 1921), *SS Princess Matokia* (May 23, 1920), and *U.S.A.T. Mercury* (June 16, 1920). You can find digitized images of the manifests online. ***www.ancestry.com***

My grandfather was a Polar Bear!

If your grandfather was a "Polar Bear", he was a World War I U.S. soldier and part of the Expedition Forces. The American military intervention at Archangel, Russia at the end of World War I was nicknamed the "Polar Bear Expedition."

> *Ostensibly sent to Russia to prevent a German advance and to help
> reopen the Eastern Front, American soldiers found themselves fighting Bolshevik
> revolutionaries for months after the Armistice ended fighting in France.*
> — Bentley Historical Library

Kneeling third from the left is Hipolit Wagner. He was inducted into the army under General Haller in 1918. Photo courtesy of Arthur A. Wagner.

After suffering through bitter winters, the soldiers returned to the States between 1920 and 1922. They left behind the bodies of their deceased comrades; but their remains were brought home for military burial in 1929. Photos of the reinterment and services held at the Polar Bear Memorial at White Chapel Cemetery in Troy, Michigan are held at the Bentley Historical Library in Ann Arbor, Michigan. The library holds the archives of the Polar Bear Association. The association, founded by the World War I veterans, continues to honor the soldiers each Memorial Day at White Chapel. ***www.bentley.umich.edu***

What if our soldier was buried overseas?

The U.S. American Battle Monuments Commission is responsible for the design, construction, operation, and maintenance of permanent American cemeteries in foreign countries. The commission administers twenty-four permanent American burial grounds on foreign soil and they have an online database where you can search for relatives. The World War I listing has the records of those casualties that are buried in their cemeteries or listed on the Walls of the Missing—a total of 33,717 records. Additionally, the World War II database has a total of 176,399 records. You can view all of the World War II Army and Air Force casualties from a specific unit or by state and cemetery. ***www.abmc.gov/home.php***

A U.S. military gravestone in Poland?

At first glance, the only atypical feature about Stanley Andronik's standard issue military tombstone (shown at right) is the addition of the crucifix. But this tombstone marks his grave in Dąbrowa Białostocka, Poland. It raises the question of how did it get there? The answer is the U.S. Military shipped it there to the family.

Census and military records identify Stanisław Andronik's life in America. Born in Jasionówka, Poland, he arrived on July 11, 1905 in New York via Antwerp. He worked at the Vulcan Iron Works and reported to the New Britain Draft Board on June 5, 1917. Stanley's tombstone was ordered from the Cemetery Division of the Graves Registration Service and the marker application can be found on NARA NY microfilm M1916. The microfilm includes all applications for World War I gravestone requests made between 1925-1941.

The U.S. military tombstone of Stanley Andronik was modified with a crucifix. Unfortunately, his surname is misspelled with an e instead of an i.

Not only are World War I gravestone orders on the film; but also orders for Civil War and Spanish American veterans. Any U.S. veteran is eligible for a military memorial. The U.S. government will ship them anywhere in the world for the unmarked grave of a soldier.

> *It is understood that the stone will be furnished and delivered at the railroad station or steamboat landing above indicated, at Government expense, freight prepaid, and agree it will be promptly received and set up at private expense.*
> — Department of Veteran Affairs

Requests are currently made to the Department of Veteran Affairs in Virginia; but in 1931 the requests were submitted to the Memorial Branch. The 8"x 5" fill-in-the-blank form included the name of the person to whom the gravestone was to be shipped and their address. The signed application was acknowledgement to accept the gravestone and to place it on the decedent's grave. The form also included the date the application was verified, the date the gravestone was ordered, who ordered it, and the date it was shipped.

To order a gravestone for a member of your family who served in the military, contact Memorial Programs Service (41A1), Department of Veteran Affairs, 5109 Russell, Quantico Road, VA, 22134-3903. *www.cem.va.gov*

What is the Old Man's Draft?

Researchers have an additional chance to find information on their immigrant ancestor if he registered for the World War II draft. The draft requiring men ages 45-64—born on or between April 28, 1877 and February 16, 1897—was known as the "Old Man's Draft".

Old Man's Draft World War II draft registration, Pennsylvania.

Information on the registration cards is more descriptive than the World War I cards. The individual's physical description gives the height in feet and inches instead of short, medium, or tall. Their weight was recorded in pounds instead of describing their build as thin, medium, or stout. Hair color, eye color, complexion, and race were recorded as well. The cards also asked for the name and address of the employer; and the name of someone who would always know his whereabouts.

These index cards have been microfilmed and are available from regional NARA archives and via your local FHC. One note to remember when viewing the films is that the initial filming was not accurate. The front of one man's card was filmed with the back of another man's information. This happened in four batches: Delaware, Maryland, Pennsylvania, and West Virginia. While that can be frustrating, it is better than if you are searching the following states, the cards of which were destroyed and never microfilmed: Alabama, Florida, Georgia, Kentucky, Mississippi, North Carolina, South Carolina, and Tennessee.

Ancestry has a database for the "Old Man's Draft." It is incomplete to date as all of the records have not been extracted. None of the states I needed were online. So, I tried a keyword search in the extracted states for the Polish village of Tczew and the Michigan village of Calumet. It returned two entries for men born in Tczew, and 284 entries for men born in Calumet, Michigan and residing in other states.

Polish Army Veterans Association of America, Inc.

PAVA is the acronym for the English title of the group Polish Army Veterans Association of America, Inc. SWAP stands for the Polish title *Stowarzyszenie Weteranów Armii Polskiej w Ameryce*. It was founded in 1921 by a returning soldier who fought in Haller's Army. World War II vets added to the membership and there are still at least 40 posts (*placówki*) in North America. *Haller's Polish Army in France* author, Paul Valasek, wrote about his visit to the headquarters in New York. Paul's complete article can be found through the following URL: *www.polishroots.com/Resources/swap_lodges/tabid/273/Default.aspx* PAVA welcomes descendants of members to join the association. There is also a Ladies Auxiliary founded in 1925. You might have a photo of your grandmother dressed in a cape with a Polish military style hat. She was a PAVA Ladies Auxiliary member.

The New York headquarters has membership applications that list the usual vital information; but also includes the unit the soldier served in and the rank he held when discharged. You can find the *placówka* to which your ancestor belonged online. *www.pava-swap.org/muzeum/folder.htm* PAVA's description of some of their holdings:

> *The headquarters maintains a library with over 18,000 membership cards and historical records on the organization of the Polish Army in France during World War I (1917-1919). We hold a unique and valuable collection of photographs from Polish military camps. Similar materials are related to the history of the Polish Army in the West during World War II, with a large and interesting photo collection on the Polish Navy. Archives include oral history and audio-video materials.*

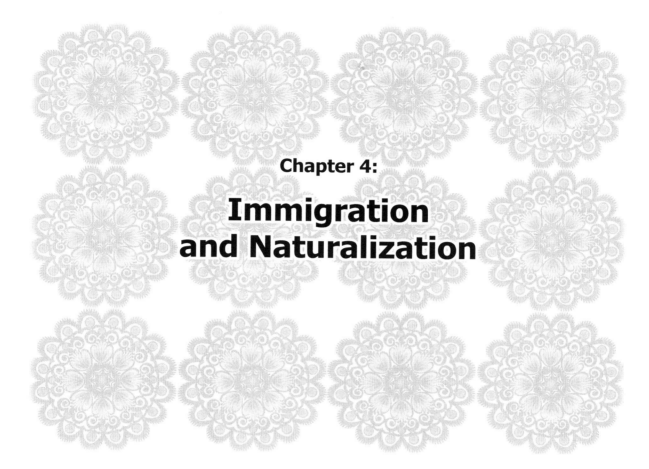

Chapter 4:

Immigration and Naturalization

The 1900 and 1920 U.S. census recorded your ancestors' approximate year of immigration and naturalization (if they became citizens). These dates can help locate the bridge documents between the United States and Poland: declarations of intent, naturalization papers, and ship manifests. You may still need the name of the Polish village from these documents to continue your research in the "old country."

Ancestors became American citizens by renouncing their allegiance to their former country and filing their intentions with the U.S. government. The Declaration of Intention (First Papers) was usually filed soon after an immigrant's arrival, while the Petition for Naturalization (Final Papers) required a waiting period, usually five years. A Certificate of Citizenship was given to the new citizen to carry; and it may have had a photo attached. The certificate's number is useful for locating other court related documents. In 1906, the U.S. government set up the Immigration and Naturalization Service (INS), which established standard forms and procedures. Citizenship papers required the names, dates and place of birth, and current residence of an applicant and his family. Between 1855 and 1922, wives and children became citizens when their husband/father did.

Where can I find Manifests and Naturalization Records?

Traditionally, manifests and naturalization papers have been obtained from microfilms, or at state and federal archives and courthouses. Once found, the documents can reveal much information. Take time to look for records of other villagers and extended family members to help you learn about the patterns of Polish migration and more about your family. The 1922 Naturalization Act stated that a woman who married an alien would lose her citizenship. She would have to go through the naturalization process to regain it. It took nine years for the law to be repealed. After 1922, women had to file their own papers.

Prior to 1906

Any "court of record" (municipal, county, state, or federal) could grant U.S. citizenship. There were no uniform procedures. The information contained in these records varies greatly from institution to institution. Few list the village of birth or the last residence in Poland. There are no centralized indices to these pre-1906 records. Contact the state archives where the naturalization occurred to request a search for the records. Some indices and records have been donated to the National Archives and are available on NARA microfilms. Indices have also been microfilmed by The Church of Jesus Christ Latter-day Saints (LDS).

After 1906

Naturalizations from Federal Courts are held in the NARA's regional facilities for the federal courts in that area. All naturalization records after September 27, 1906 have duplicate copies filed at: U.S. Citizenship and Immigration Services (USCIS), FOIA/PA Section, Room 5304 425 Eye Street NW, Washington, DC 20536; (202) 514-1554.

Current online sites are now adding indices and scanned images of these documents. Indices have become available via archives, libraries, and several fee-based Web sites. Three popular sites, Ancestry, Footnote, and World Vital Records, have indexes and some scanned images of naturalization papers. Although requiring subscription, these Web sites may be accessed for free at a local FHC or public library. *www.ancestry.com*; *www.footnote.com*; *www.worldvitalrecords.com*

Genealogy Program

The U.S. Citizenship and Immigration Services launched their fee-based Genealogy Program in late 2007. Records available through the USCIS Genealogy Program include: Naturalization Certificate Files (C-files); Alien Registration Forms from August 1, 1940 to March 31, 1944; Visa files from July 1, 1924 to March 31, 1944; Registry Files from March 2, 1929 to March 31, 1944; Alien Files (A-files) numbered below 8 million (A8000000) and documents therein dated prior to May 1, 1951. Also available on the Web site is the USCIS Genealogy Program brochure. *www.uscis.gov/genealogy*

3911

UNITED STATES OF AMERICA

ORIGINAL

PETITION FOR NATURALIZATION

To the Honorable the *Supreme* Court, *New York, Erie County*

The petition of *Emil Stachurski* hereby filed, respectfully showeth:

First. My place of residence is *19 Elmwood Ave, Depew, N. Y.*

Second. My occupation is *Crane Operator*

Third. I was born on the *15th* day of *August* anno Domini 1*887* at *Ratoszyn, Poland, Russia*

Fourth. I emigrated to the United States from *Bremen, Germany* on or about the *8th* day of *March* anno Domini 1*906* and arrived in the United States, at the port of *Baltimore, Md.* on the *24th* day of *March* anno Domini 1*906* on the vessel *Cassel*

Fifth. I declared my intention to become a citizen of the United States on the *21st* day of *October* anno Domini 1*913* at *Buffalo, N. Y.* in the *Supreme* Court of *New York, Erie County*

Sixth. I am married. My wife's name is *Helena Stachurski* She was born in *Belavoda, Poland, Russia* and now resides at *19 Elmwood Ave, Depew, N. Y.*

I have *two* children, and the name, date and place of birth, and place of residence of each of said children is as follows:

Alfred Stachurski born March 29, 1913, in Depew, N. Y.

Leonora Stachurski, born October 5, 1915 in Depew, N. Y.

Emiljan, later known as Emil, filed his 1913 Petition for Naturalization at the Federal Court of Erie County in Buffalo, New York.

The naturalization document represented above did provide the name of the last place of residence in Poland for both Emil and his wife, Helena Jaszczyńska. They married in the United States; but both were from Russian Poland. Emiljan was born in Ratoszyn, Chodel, Lublin and Helena in Białowoda (written as Belavoda), Opole Lubelskie, Lublin.

Code	Party Name	Group	Date	Status
R	Stachurski, Alfred	CITZ	11/09/1915	B
D	Stachurski, Emil	CITZ	11/09/1915	B
R	Stachurski, Helena	CITZ	11/09/1915	B
R	Stachurski, Lenora	CITZ	11/09/1915	B

Above are the search results for Stachurski in the Erie County Clerk's (New York) database. Their online site for login public view requires a readily created userid and password. *http://ecclerk.erie.gov:9080/prod_public_view/login.jsp*
The database lists Emil's wife and children, who became citizens under his petition. Code "D" is for the declarant, code "R" is for the wife and children, while "B" indicates the data was imported from computer systems older than August 1, 2005. Information was requested in writing and mailed by the Erie County Clerk's Office, 25 Delaware Avenue, Buffalo, NY 14202.

How do you find your ancestors' passenger ship manifest?

Previous research may have provided the name of your ancestor's village in Poland; but most researchers want the ship manifest to verify each person's passage. The easiest way to search for the passage is to put the given and surnames in their proper Polish form. There is an urban legend that names were changed by intolerant Ellis Island officials. Immigrants changed names informally or via probate court for political, economic, and religious reasons. Did the family anglicize their names in the U.S.? Estelle Adamski traveled as Stanislawa Adamska, James Voight as Jakub Wojtkowiak, and Joseph Halper arrived as Jossel Dobroniewski from Białystok. Consult the Polish Genealogical Society of America publications *Polish Surnames: Origins and Meanings*, by William F. Hoffman and *First Names of the Polish Commonwealth: Origins & Meanings*, by William F. Hoffman and George W. Helon, for spelling variations.

The books list first and last names in Polish and include variations of the names in German, Hebrew, Latin, Polish, Russian, and Ukrainian. The primer on the Polish language makes the researcher aware that the Polish alphabet has 32 letters, 9 vowels, 23 consonants; and that q, v, and x are not normally used. The additional letters with diacriticals (marks on the letters)—ą, ć; ę, ł, ń, ó, ś, ź, and ż—can be, and were often, misinterpreted. Unaware, transcribers of the Ellis Island database entered the given name Władysław as Wtadystaw. The surname Zdziebko is often listed as Fdziebko because the Z was written in the European manner with a short horizontal crossbar added through the middle.

Where can I find passenger list information?

Traditionally, indexes and manifests have been obtained via microfilm from NARA and LDS. But many Web sites are now offering digitized images and indices. If you choose to look at traditional microfilms, I would still recommend use of the internet to confirm which microfilms are available. Joe Beine offers superb links for determining what film number corresponds to the manifest information you are seeking. His introduction states: *"This is a listing of indexes of passenger lists (also called immigration records or ship manifests) for ships that sailed to the United States from 1820 to the 1940's, including microfilm, CD-ROMs, books, and online indexes. Microfilm records listed here are available from the National Archives (NARA) and some of its branches. Most are also available from LDS Family History Centers. Some public libraries (especially genealogy libraries) may also carry passenger lists from the National Archives microfilm, which can be viewed online at Ancestry. If you are only interested in the microfilmed passenger lists for offline research see: National Archives Passenger Lists on*

Microfilm." www.germanroots.com/passengers.html

Some of the key ports and time frames for which passenger lists are available include:

New York (1820-1957)	Baltimore (1820-1952)	Boston (1820-1943)
Philadelphia (1800-1945)	New Orleans (1820-1945)	Galveston (1846-1948)

Ancestry has all of the U.S. ports indexed in a text database and linked to images of the manifests and ships. Additionally, the Texas Seaport Museum has compiled a computerized listing of immigrants to Galveston, Texas called the *Galveston Immigration Database.*
www.galvestonhistory.org/Galveston_Immigration_Database.asp

A useful site to learn the history of immigration is *TheShipsLists*. This Web site has immigration reports, newspaper records, shipwreck information, ship pictures, ship descriptions, and shipping-line fleet lists. You can view hundreds of passenger lists to Canada, the United States, and Australia. *www.theshipslist.com*

What are St. Albans Lists?

St. Albans Lists are the collective records of mostly European immigrants who crossed the border, whether by land or sea, from Canada into the United States between 1895 and 1954. (Canadian born immigrants were not recorded on the St. Albans Lists until 1906). A large number of ancestors arrived at Canadian ports including Quebec, Halifax, Saint Johns, and North Sydney. They continued their journey to the U.S. via train or ferry boats, with St. Albans, Vermont being only one of many portals of entry. The Immigration and Naturalization Service (INS) records were originally filed in Montreal's INS office. When the INS moved their offices and records to St. Albans, this particular manifest collection developed its name. Information in this database generally includes: name, age, birth date, birthplace, gender, ethnicity/nationality, last residence, vessel or airline name, and ports of arrival and departure, and arrival date.

What about the Detroit Border Crossings and Passenger Crew Lists?

Ancestry has created an online database of aliens crossing from Canada and entering the United States through the port of Detroit, Michigan from 1905-1957. The information provided will vary over the years simply because of the variety of forms that were utilized to collect the original information.

Steve Morse One-Step Webpages

Steve Morse has developed his *One-Step Webpages* to streamline the hunt for the manifests. His Ellis Island Gold Form (1892-1924) allows for "sounds like" searches and uses the Daitch-Mokotoff Soundex, which is better able to handle the sounds and spellings of Eastern European names. The Web site allows for searches at all possible U.S. ports, not just New York. The site also allows for searches by town, so you can find other villagers who came to the U.S. Use the "TOWN" field to bring up smaller towns and villages in the U.S. that Poles were returning to, such as Stevens Point, Ironwood, Hammond, or Perth Amboy. When names are misspelled, the village may be the only way to locate the passenger: Polish immigrant Władysław Wilmowicz, indexed as Nladislaus Nilmouriez, was found only after a search for the name of his birth village, Mestin. ***www.stevemorse.org***

Are there departure port records?

Departure ports for Poles included Bremen, Hamburg, Stettin, and to a lesser degree, Antwerp and Rotterdam. Some traveled by land and ferry to England and departed from a British port. There are a few fragments of Stettin manifests. These surviving passenger departure lists are presently only available in the Vorpommersches Landesarchiv in Greifswald, Germany. They are available for the years 1871, 1876-1891, and 1896-1898 (other years are lost). You may write to the archive for information about researching these lists:

Landesarchiv Greifswald
Martin-Andersen-Nexö-Platz 1
D 17489 Greifswald, Deutschland
03834 5953-0.

You might also contact researcher Friedrich R. Wollmershäuser, who has an index to these lists. Herr Wollmershäuser charges a fee for researching these records. For details, see his Web site. ***www.anthonj.de/genealogen***

Bremen

Seven million emigrants sailed from Bremerhaven between 1832 and 1974. Unfortunately, all lists from 1875 to 1908 were intentionally destroyed to save space in the Bremen Archives. With the exception of 3,017 passenger lists for the years 1920-1939, all other lists were lost in World War II. The saved lists were stored in a salt mine at Bernburg an der Saale in 1942 and were transferred into the custody of the Moscow Archives at the end of World War II. The lists were returned to the Bremen Chamber of Commerce and are indexed. The online site is in both German and English. ***www.passagierlisten.de***

Header and questions on the Hamburg manifest (Verzeichniss or Register) for 1896: "Listing of the persons who have been engaged by the undersigned for emigration to Baltimore, and [will travel] on the steamship Italia, captain Fröhlich under the German flag to Baltimore. Departure of the ship on 28 August 1896."

Hamburg

Hamburg Direct and Indirect Passenger Lists and Indexes (1850-1934) are available on microfilm and through Ancestry. The database is indexed for 1885-1914. The handwritten indexes can be browsed page by page for the years 1855-1934.

Below are the questions and answers for a family traveling from Hamburg to Baltimore in 1896. Anton Przytula was in the company of his grandmother and aunt. Their names were listed together with a bracket indicating the family unit.

1. Zuname/Surname: Przytula
2. Vornamen/Given Name: Antony
3. Geschlecht/Gender männlich/male, weiblich/female: Male
4. Alter/Age: 4
5. Bisheriger Wohnort/Previous Residence: Groß Lensk
6. Im Staate resp. in der Provinz/State or Province: Ostpreußen
7. Bisheriger Stand oder Beruf/Occupation or social standing: Kind/Child
8. Ziel der Auswanderung (Ort und Land sind anzugeben)/Destination: Baltimore
9. Zahl der Personen/Number of Persons: 3
10. Erwachsene und Kinder über 10 Jahre/Adults & Children Over 10 years
    Kinder/Children: 1
11. Unter 10 Jahr/Under 10 years: 2
12. Unter 1 Jahr/Under 1 year: 0

The first page of the two page manifest of Edmond's journey on the S.S. Lapland sailing from Antwerp on May 8, 1909. Questions 1-12 are on the first page of the manifest.

The voice of Edmond Stachurski (1892-2000)

Edmond Stachurski of Ajax, North Carolina was one of the immigrants who told his memories of the voyage. The interview was conducted by Janice Levine, oral historian with the Ellis Island Immigration Museum. The transcript is held at the Ellis Island Recording Studio. His narrative expands the short answers asked on the Antwerp-New York voyage. Read his words and imagine it was written by your grandfather. As of 2007, Levine was still seeking passengers who disembarked at Ellis Island from 1892 through 1954.

Manifest Page 1

1. No. on list: 26

2. Name in Full - Family Name, Given name: *Stachurski, Edmond*

3. Age Yrs.: 17. *"I was born on June 22, 1892."*

4. Sex: *Male*

5. Married or single: *Single*

6. Calling or Occupation: Laborer. *"My mother died when I was four or five. I was sent to work at my Godmother's to help out in the blacksmith shop. I helped her husband with the blacksmith work. This helped me later on to work at another blacksmith shop where my stepmother placed me when Dad left for America. I stayed there about four years helping the blacksmith and doing farm chores to sustain my upkeep. I also helped around a windmill for my uncle Emil while he was away at times."*

7. Able to – Read what language: No/No. *"I use to write very good – reading and writing by taking Russian."*

8. Nationality (County of which citizen or subject): Russian. *"Since I was a Russian subject I had to get a Russian permit to go to Austria to visit my cousins. I lied. I had a difficult time getting a permit because I was of age to serve in the Russian army."*

9. Race or people: *Polish*

10. Last Permanent residence Country, City or Town: Wico. *"I was born in Opole, Lublin. I left Boby-wieś* [ed. note: This is a good example of how a village name is inaccurate and several

The second page of Edmond's manifest and the arrival in New York on May 17, 1909.
Questions 13-29 are listed on the second page of the manifest.

sources are needed to confirm the home village], *for Depew, New York. I [had] learned by heart, Depew, 66 Penora which I can never forget now today. The train stopped way out in a field somewhere."*

14. Whether having a ticket to such final destination: *"I was placed on a train to travel for a day and night from New York City to Depew. I was left off the train in the middle of nowhere. But, little by little, I kept on till I found my way to 66 Penora Street, where Dad and Stepmother lived. No one who was on the train knew what a banana or tomato [given to them at Ellis Island for the journey] was so all in fun they threw them at each other."*

15. By whom was passage paid (whether alien, how paid his own passage, whether paid by relative, whether paid by another person, or by any corporation, society, municipality, society, or government): *"Father Dad, Ignacy, while in America, sent a ticket to my stepmother and little by little Dad sent for us all. Finally, Dad sent me a ticket and a few dollars to board a liner to America. I was about 16 ½ years. I'll never forget it was April, 1909."*

16. Whether in possession of $50, and if less, how much?: *"Five, five dollars, Russian money, gold. They warned me in a letter before I come don't tell everybody you got money."*

18. Whether going to join a relative or friend, and if so, what relative or friend, and his complete name and address: *"When I reached 66 Penora it was a very big disappointment to me, I only found mother, second mother. My Stepmother kept four boarders. Two worked on the day shift, and two on the night shift. All four shared one bedroom with one double bed. Dad said this way the bed was kept warm. There was no room for me there. I was too young to get a shop job, no language skill, no home, no money and the big question was what to do. I was advised to go to Perry, NY, to work in the cotton mill because they hired under age (16 ½) workers. It was here in Perry that I met my brother Emil and my sister Victoria."*

Questions 21-27 [Deal with health and character] Conditions of health mental and physical: Good health, 4' 11", fair complexion, light hair, dark eyes. *"On the 8th day the ship stopped and we had to stay on the ship till we got shots and were examined as to who was healthy or sick. We received information and were numbered to our destination."*

Interpreting Passenger List Annotations

Passenger lists created after 1892 frequently have a variety of markings, codes, and annotations in the margins and columns. Marian L. Smith, historian for the U.S. Immigration and Naturalization Service, with the assistance of Elise Friedman, Flora Gursky, and Eleanor Bien, have published online *"A Guide to Interpreting Passenger List Annotations."* Find out if your ancestors were detained, ill, or thought to be a "Likely Public Charge", or LPC. ***www.jewishgen.org/infofiles/Manifests/occ***

Are there any other stories about the passage?

Several books come to mind and include *Island of Hope, Island of Tears* by David M. Brownstone, Irene M. Franck, and Douglas Brownstone, 2000; and *Ellis Island Interviews* by Peter Morton Coan, 2004. Both are based on interviews with Europeans who traveled to the U.S. between 1892 and 1930. Additionally, books such as John S. Kramek's 1990 *Refugee's Trails* documents his exile as a Polish child to Siberia during World War II and his passage to the United States via Bombay. He describes the voyage of over 700 displaced persons on the U.S. naval destroyer, *USS Hermitage,* and the attack by Japanese submarines as they passed through enemy waters.

Heinz Chinnow, born in 1931 in Stolpmünde, Stolp, Pommern (now Ustka, Słupsk, Poland), relates his World War II journey in the book *Pomerania: 1945 Echoes of the Past*. As a young German boy forced out of his village by the approaching Russian forces, his family fled their Baltic fishing village on his father's trawler. His diary entries include the precise navigation required of his father to avoid the Russian mines in the sea. Heinz came to the United States in 1957 with his new bride, Klaere; their manifest of arrival is indexed on Ancestry. Reflecting post-war immigration, they arrived in New York aboard a Flying Tiger Line, Inc. DC-6 operated by the Great Lakes Airlines.

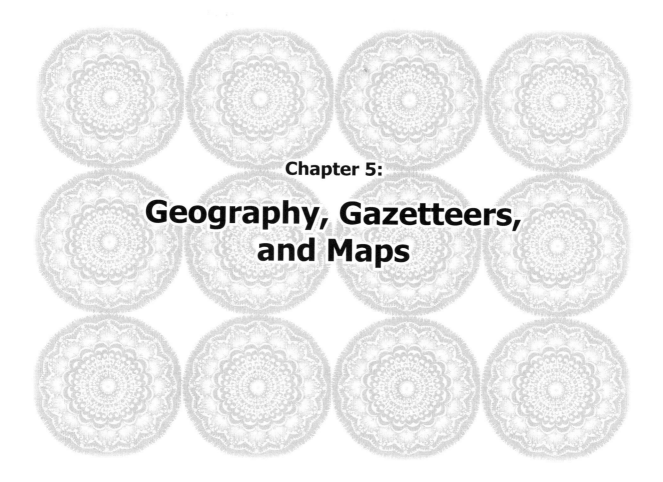

Chapter 5:

Geography, Gazetteers, and Maps

Whether it is finding the family village on an 1850s map or the changing borders of partitioned Poland, maps are indispensable. A range of sources, types, and uses of maps exist. Universities and libraries have digitized vintage maps that reference the old German, Austrian, and Russian partitions of Poland. There are also interactive maps with English and Polish interfaces of the modern counties of Poland. The online collections make it easy to access maps of the time period you are researching. You can compare the period and current maps to see the ancestral village location and determine if the community still exists. A careful study may reveal that the village has merged with other villages or was incorporated into a larger town or city.

The *Słownik Geograficzny Królestwa Polskiego (Geographical Dictionary of the Kingdom of Poland)* is a 15-volume gazetteer that was published between 1880 and 1902 under the direction of Filip Sulimierski. It is one cornerstone of a good Polish research library and is now available on CD through PGSA or online. Extracts from a translation for the region of Kaszuby and the village of Puck follow the synopsis of the słownik/dictionary.

What was my ancestors' village like?

The słownik is just the publication you need to learn about your ancestor's village. Noted researcher and professor, Rafał T. Prinke, explains what makes the *Słownik Geograficzny Królestwa Polskiego i innych krajów słowiańskich (SGKP)* unique:

> There are many reference works indispensable for researching Polish local history and genealogy, but none of them can be compared to the SGKP. This remarkable achievement of late 19th century Polish scholarship remains unmatched, and not only by anything in Poland—no project of similar scope has ever been completed for other countries. Every entry contains (to a varying degree of detail) all available information including detailed description of a given place in the late 19th century, including: geographic and administrative (both political and church—for all denominations) placement, demographic, social, religious and other statistics; schools, industry, communication, agriculture, trade; historical survey—foundation, important events; names of successive owners; names of inhabitants; and a bibliography with all relevant books and articles.

The following two entries were translated by William F. Hoffman and presented with his permission.

Słownik entry for Kaszuby:

In form the Kaszuby is not tall; he is bony, nimble, of rather fair complexion, usually with light-colored hair. The men's clothing consists of a long, pleated frock (of homespun), with firm calf's leather shoes, often tar-soaked, and pants, also of homespun, reaching down to their tops. Currently the most typical feature of every Kaszub's attire is a large cap (like the ones firemen wear), covering the back of the skull, and the ears with flaps; gray sheepskin is sewn on the front, and the inside is also lined with sheepskin. They used to wear a tall sheepskin cap with short silk ribbons, usually yellow, on the back. Young Kaszub women also delight in warm homespun dresses with similar ribbons. In summer they wear on their heads a thin white scarf knotted under the chin-thus they are called białki ["white ones"], vol. 3, pp. 904-907.

Słownik entry for the village of Puck:

The village of Puck is called Peck in Kaszubian, Putzig in German. There is a 3rd-class post office, a district court, a Catholic church and a Protestant one (1780), a synagogue, a three-grade Catholic school, a two-grade Protestant school, a tax office, several distilleries and brickyards, a windmill, a steam mill, and several breweries. Puck beer was once famous. Belonging to the municipal gmina are the farmstead Heinrichshof, the forestry station Kepino, the Prangenthal brickyard, the Seefeld steam mill, and the farmstead Tannenberg. In 1869 there were 2,357 inhabitants (1,589 Catholics, 664 Protestants, 102 Jews, and 2 dissidents); in 1880 there were 2,019 inhabitants; in 1885 there were 1,880 inhabitants and 163 houses. The climate is harsh, marine, and healthy; the soil is unusually fertile. The inhabitants are employed mainly in fishing and retail trade. There are four fairs yearly, two with booths and two for cattle. The town's coat of arms features a lion atop a silver salmon.

Zbliż	Szukaj w sieci
○ 2 m	
○ 4 m	Szukaj
● 8 m	
○ 16 m	**Pokaż na mapie**
○ 32 m	Miejscowość
○ 64 m	
○ 128 m	
○ 256 m	Ulica / plac / aleja
○ 512 m	
○ kontur	
Oddal	Zaawansowane Pokaż
Środkuj	Drukuj Zapisz Pomóż

Where is Pacanów?

In one adventure of the cartoon character Koziołek Matołek—a slow-witted but brave billy goat quite famous in Poland—Koziołek is on a quest to find Pacanów, where they make goat shoes. Little did he know that his quest could have been streamlined by using an online map. The Web site uses the latest technology to pinpoint a location in modern Poland. The search box is easy to use once the Polish commands are identified. ***www.mapa.szukacz.pl***

Polish	English	Polish	English
Szukaj w sieci	Search the net	Ulica/plac/aleja	Street/Place/Avenue
Szukaj	Search	Pokaż	Display/Find
Pokaż na mapie	Make a map	Zbliż	Zoom In
Miejscowość	Location: town or place	Oddal	Zoom Out
Drukuj	Print	Zapisz	Write
Odległość	Distance Tool	Pomóż	Help
Środkuj	Center (to center town on screen)	Zaawansowane	Advanced
współrzędne	Longitude and latitude	Opis	Description

The results for Pacanów show two locations. Koziołek sought: Pacanów wieś (village); woj. świętokrzyskie (province of Świętokrzyskie); pow. buski (county of Busko-Zdrój); and gmina Pacanów (district of Pacanów).

Current maps and atlases are also useful. The Marco Polo *Polska Atlas Drogowy (Road Atlas of Poland)* includes 236 pages of maps (1:200,000), eight regional maps (1:000,000), 65 city maps (1:20,000), as well as four general maps of Central Europe. They are in color and indexed. The index from the first edition has been reprinted by Genealogy Unlimited and offers the 1975-1998 administrative districts the Family History Library used to catalog the microfilms of Poland. *Höfer Verlag* (Germany) offers maps of Poland. The former Prussian locations have bilingual labels with the current Polish name and previous German name. This makes cross-referencing the location much easier.

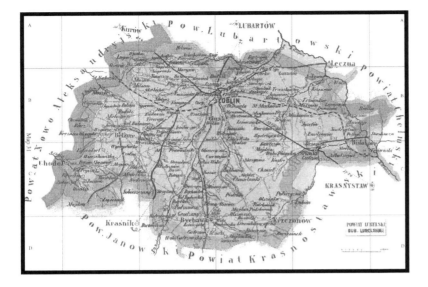

*The powiat of Łomża
in the gubernia of
Łomża from
J.M. Bazewicz's
"The Illustrated Geographic Atlas
of the Kingdom of Poland"
published in Warsaw
in 1907, page 41.*

Where was Russian Poland?

Russian Poland was also known as Congress Poland or the Kingdom of Poland. This area of Poland was under Russian imperial rule from 1814-1915. Its population increased to 6.1 million in 1870 and 10 million in 1900. Ancestors might cite their place of birth as one of the larger cities in Russian Poland such as Płock, Łomża, Białystok, Warszawa, or Lublin. They are more likely to have come from villages or shtetls such as Kuczbork, Posadów, or Iłża (Driltsh in Yiddish). A shtetl was typically a small town with a large Jewish population.

One of the best collections of maps of Russian Poland is *Atlas Geograficzny Illustrowany Królestwa Polskiego (The Illustrated Geographic Atlas of the Kingdom of Poland)* published by J. M. Bazewicz in Warsaw (1907). It is held by libraries in the United States including Wayne State University, University of Chicago, New York Public Library, and Harvard University. The Polish Genealogical Society of America (PGSA) has scanned the maps from the atlas and they are available online. ***www.pgsa.org/Maps/polishatlas.php***

The maps were updated with coordinates so that they could be indexed. The atlas is also available in three formats at the Family History Library in Salt Lake City: Reference Book 943.8 E3b; microfilm 0873665 (item 3); and microfiche 6000827. It was printed with color lithographs and has illustrations of interest to family historians. Illustrations include the Pałac w Pojeziorach (Palace in Pojeziory) and Ratusz (townhall) in Radom. Figures of people identified as "typical of the region" are pictured from Ostrołęka, the Kalisz region, and Kalwaria.

Additionally, the Federation of East European Family History Societies (FEEFHS) has an online map titled *The Polish Provinces of the Russian Empire 1902.* ***www.feefhs.org/maplibrary/russian/re-polan.html***

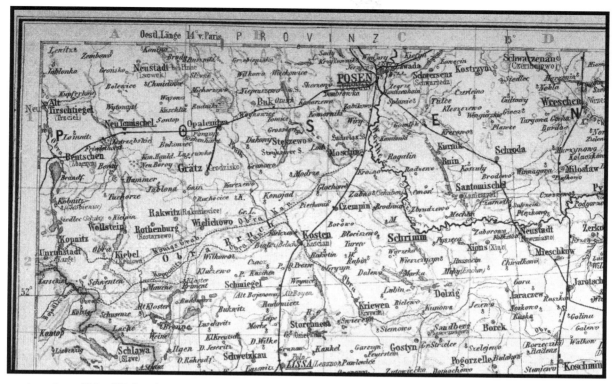

A section of Map VI C1 of Province of Posen from the Ludwig Ravenstein's "1883 Atlas of the German Empire."

Where was Prussia?

The Polish provinces of Prussia included: East Prussia, known in German as Ostpreußen spelled with the double s (an esset) and called Prusy Wschodnie in Polish; West Prussia (German: Westpreußen) referred to as Prusy Zachodnie in Polish; the Province of Posen (German: Provinz Posen) will be listed in Polish documents as Prowincja Poznańska; Silesia (German: Provinz Schlesien) is Prowincja Śląska in Polish; and part of the Province of Pomerania (German: Provinz Pommern) became Poland's Województwo Pomorskie after World War II.

The *Atlas des Deutschen Reichs* is a digitized version of Ludwig Ravenstein's *1883 Atlas of the German Empire.* It is held in the collections of the University of Wisconsin-Madison Library. ***www.library.wisc.edu/etext/ravenstein/home.html***
The Web site has a map reproduced from the original title page which depicts the area covered by the *Atlas des Deutschen Reichs.* The entire map is divided into nine sections and two smaller maps of the original atlas. The online edition has further divisions to facilitate downloading. At ***www.adobe.com*** you can download the free Adobe Reader to view the online PDF files. The map's large scale (1:850,000) and gazetteer of place names help locate small towns and villages. The Map Legend (*Erklärung*) is located on the lower right corner

map (Map.9: F5-M9). The atlas is color coded and the locations of churches are marked. An accompanying table gives statistics on the religious denominations found throughout the German Empire down to the *Regierungsbezirk* and *Kreis* governmental units. The sample map (see page 55) illustrates Tulce, Schroda, Provinz Posen on Map VI C1. The 1880 statistics listed in the atlas (*Statistische Übersicht des Deutschen Reichs*) for Schroda: Konfessionen (Religions)— Protestanten (Protestant) 7574; Katholiken (Catholic) 44,089; Andre Konf (other religions) 122; Juden 848.

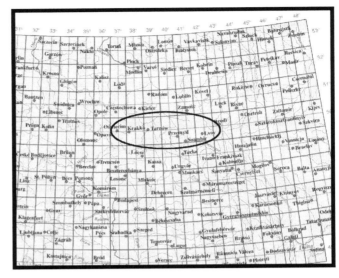

Section of the index sheet for the map set entitled 3rd Military Mapping Survey of Austria-Hungary. It is a general map of Central Europe c. 1910 with 267 sheets available online.

Where was Galicia?

Galicia was a historical region once part of the Austro-Hungarian Empire, covering territory currently divided between southern Poland and Ukraine. The name changes slightly with the regional languages: Galicja in Polish, Galician in German, and Galitzia in Yiddish. Ethnic Polish ancestors coming from this region may be listed as "Austrian." They may list their birthplace as one of the major cities such as Lviv (Polish: Lwów, German: Lemberg), Kraków (German: Krakau, Yiddish: Kruke), or Przemyśl (Ukrainian: Peremyshl, German: Prömsel). In most cases, they were from outlying villages.

Do not confuse this Galicia with a region of the same name located on the Iberian peninsula in Spain. The Polish Galician region had a varied ethnic mix: Poles, Ruthenians (Ukrainians), Germans, Armenians, Jews, Hungarians, and Romanians.

The Eötvös Loránd University's Department of Cartography and Geoinformatics in Hungary has historic maps online for Galician researchers. These are part of a series of digital maps of Austria-Hungary. The map scale is 1:200,000 and the downloadable jpg files average 3.5 MB, allowing a researcher the ability to identify churches and the layout of villages. *http://lazarus.elte.hu/hun/gb/maps.htm*

Dave Obee, owner of Genealogy Unlimited and an online vendor of Eastern European maps, reminds researchers to be cautious of Soviet Union maps (including Ukraine) printed between 1930 and 1990. The Soviet Union falsified virtually all public maps of the country, misplacing rivers and streets, distorting boundaries, and omitting geographical features.

What part of Poland does my surname come from?

It would be great if your surname was Łańcucki and you could be sure to find your ancestral records in Łańcut. Toponymic surnames are derived from the place where the original bearer lived or held land and suggests a location. Fred Hoffman's Polish surnames book lists eight pages of surnames that reference an actual location in Poland. But relying solely on the toponymic can take you on a wild goose chase, as many locations share the same name. Since surnames that reference a location may not lead you in the right direction, try the Moikrewni genealogy

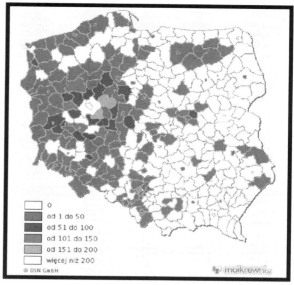

Distribution of the surname Wojtkowiak based on Professor K. Rymut's Dictionary of Surnames in Current Use in Poland at the Beginning of the 21st Century.

Web site. It offers an online tool allowing researchers to build a surname distribution map. The database contains more than 300,000 names and is color coded to identify the name in all the districts. Results vary with the absence or presence of Polish diacritical marks. ***www.moikrewni.pl/mapa***

Hoffman posted some background information regarding the source of Moikrewni's data to the Polish-Roots email list. Data was taken from the CD-ROM titled *Dictionary of Surnames in Current Use in Poland at the Beginning of the 21st Century,* compiled by Professor Kazimierz Rymut. Hoffman worked with Professor Rymut on the CD and knows the information was taken directly from the database of the PESEL Government Information Center. He explains that the office is roughly comparable to the Social Security Administration in the United States; its data is probably the most reliable to be found for Polish citizens. He feels Rymut's CD, and therefore Moikrewni, is quite dependable. Incidentally, the 1990 version of Rymut's work is available online. ***www.herby.com.pl***

So, if you want to know how widespread your surname is in Poland, enter your name in the box **SZUKAJ** (Search) or click the first letter of the name in the Moikrewni navigation bar. Move the mouse over the map to see the name of the districts. The top three locations for my ancestral surname, Wojtkowiak, included: Gostyń (398), Poznań (359), and Kościan (291). The tool returned the statistics that there are 6,435 people named Wojtkowiak in Poland today. Most live in the province of Poznań. The Moikrewni site can also generate links to create variations of the map to see how widespread your name is in Austria, Germany, and Switzerland.

Searching for Town CUTSBURG
(D-M code 547950 OR 447950)
Run on Sunday 13 May 2007 at 16:35:44
For an online Map click on Expediamaps or MapQuest or MUltimap or Google Maps

Town (Native names in BOLD)	Coordinates	Maps	Country	Distance/Direction from reference point
Gać Warcka, Gać Wartska	51°40' 18°32'	E M U G	Poland	112.4 miles WSW of Warszawa 52°15' 21°0'
Haaseberg, Zajączki, Haasenberg	53°34' 19°53'	E M U G	Poland	102.1 miles NNW of Warszawa 52°15' 21°0'
Herzberg, **Milocin**	54°17' 18°50'	E M U G	Poland	166.5 miles NNW of Warszawa 52°15' 21°0'
Jecpark, **Jedzbark**, Hirschberg	53°48' 20°46'	E M U G	Poland	107.5 miles N of Warszawa 52°15' 21°0'
Kasperki	49°33' 19°02'	E M U G	Poland	205.1 miles SSW of Warszawa 52°15' 21°0'
Koseberg, Schönhausen, **Kozia Góra**	53°52' 20°05'	E M U G	Poland	117.9 miles NNW of Warszawa 52°15' 21°0'
Krzywy Róg, Krummenort	53°46' 21°18'	E M U G	Poland	105.5 miles N of Warszawa 52°15' 21°0'
Kucbork, Kutzburg	53°27' 20°55'	E M U G	Poland	82.9 miles N of Warszawa 52°15' 21°0'
Kuczbork	53°05' 20°03'	E M U G	Poland	69.9 miles NW of Warszawa 52°15' 21°0'
Kuczbork	53°05' 20°02'	E M U G	Poland	70.3 miles NW of Warszawa 52°15' 21°0'
Kurzebrack, Kurzybrak, **Korzeniewo**	53°45' 18°52'	E M U G	Poland	136.3 miles NW of Warszawa 52°15' 21°0'
Żadzbork, Sensburg, **Mrągowo**	53°52' 21°18'	E M U G	Poland	112.3 miles N of Warszawa 52°15' 21°0'

Number of matches = 12

Search results for the town of Cutsburg using the ShtetlSeeker.

What do I do when the village name is not on a map?

The ancestral village identified by oral tradition or on a U.S. document is often misspelled. Jewish Gen's *ShtetlSeeker* is an online village seeking tool that uses the Daitch-Mokotoff Soundex system. ***www.jewishgen.org/Communities***

This Soundex system was designed with the phonetics of Slavic, Germanic, and Yiddish names in mind. The search engine creates a phonetic rendition of the name being searched, and compares it to names within the database to generate suggested geographic locations in a range of 31 Central and Eastern European countries; plus, all of the former Soviet republics and Turkey. The locations are further identified by the distance and/or direction from the country's capital city providing longitude and latitude. Links are provided to modern online maps: *Expedia, Google, Mapquest,* and *Multimap.*

Additional *ShtetlSeeker* features include the "Radius Search", which allows you to enter a specific longitude and latitude and request surrounding villages within a set radius (kilometers or miles). Searches can be further customized by indicating the first letter of a village. This is very helpful when looking for the misspelled village of a spouse who was from a nearby village.

Galician Town Locator Search Results

Town	Admin District	Gmina	Roman Catholic	Jewish	Greek Catholic
Zarzecze	Bohorodczany	Solotwina	Solotwina	Solotwina	Solotwina
Zarzecze	Jaroslau (Jaroslaw)	Jaroslau	Zarzecze	Jaroslau	Pelnatycze
Zarzecze	Jaslo	Jaslo	Dembowiec	Jaslo	--
Zarzecze	Mosciska	Sadowa Wisznia	Sadowa Wisznia	Sadowa Wisznia	Tuliglowy
Zarzecze	Nadwórna	Delatyn	Delatyn	Delatyn	Zarzecze
Zarzecze	Neusandez (Nowy Sacz)	Altsandez (Stary Sacz)	Lacko	Altsandez	--
Zarzecze	Nisko	Ulanów	Raclawice	Ulanów	Dabrówka
Zarzecze	Rzeszów	Rzeszów	Lubenia	Czudec (BH. Strzyzów)	--
Zarzecze	Saybusch (Zywiec)	Saybusch	Saybusch	Zablocie	--
Zarzecze	Zloczów	Zloczów	Zloczów	Zloczów	Zloczów

Search results for the town of Zarzecze using the Galician Town Locator.

What is a Gazetteer?

A gazetteer is a geographic dictionary index. It typically contains information concerning the geographic makeup of a country or region, and the social statistics and population. Useful for genealogical purposes, it lists the location of the civil records office, regional religions, and their churches and temples. Gazetteers can be found in reference sections of most libraries. Two useful online gazetteers that can help researchers identify their ancestral village in Galicia (Austrian Poland) and Prussia (German Poland) will be described further.

The first is the *Galician Town Locator* that can be found on online. Researchers may encounter another brick wall after finding the correct spelling of their ancestral village. Many villages throughout the country share the same name. The site helps pinpoint the correct village by sorting out the Polish terms for administrative subdivisions: *Województwo* (province) *Powiat* (county) and *Gmina* (township, district). The locator information was extracted from a gazetteer compiled by the Austro-Hungarian Empire (*Gemeindelexikon der im Reichsrate vertretenen Königreiche und Länder*). It lists the locations (*Standorte*) of Roman Catholic, Greek Catholic, and Jewish records. ***www.polishroots.org***

Uwe-Karsten Krickhahn hosts *Kartenmeister* (German for "Map master"). *Kartenmeister* is a comprehensive resource to find the German/Polish name changes for the German provinces of: East Prussia, West Prussia, Posen, Pomerania, and Silesia. It currently lists most towns and geographic features: mills, some bridges, battlefields, named trees, cenotaphs, etc. You can search by the German name or the current Polish, Russian, or Lithuanian name. ***www.Kartenmeister.com***

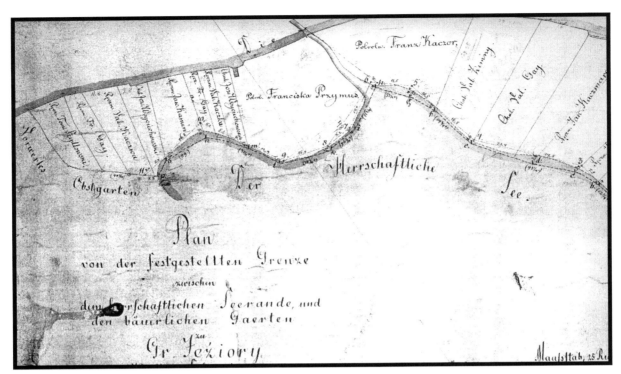

*Plan of the border established between the lake shore belonging to the lord's estate
and the peasant garden at Groß Jeziory in Schroda county. May, 1852.*

Are there maps of landowners?

Many archives maintain finding aids and catalogs in traditional card catalogs and binders and these collections may not be listed in their online catalog.

The map above was obtained during a research visit to the Archiwum Państwowe in Poznań. The archivist was asked about materials not filmed by the Family History Library that would be of interest to a family historian. Maps showing the land granted to peasants when manors were divided are known as "separation maps." Some archives also hold the documentation to this process.

Identified on the map above are the landholders, including Półrolnicy ("half-farmers"): Franciska Przymus, Franz Kaczor, Tom. Szydłowski; Chałupniks (cottagers): Fr. Gay, Joz. Woyciechowski, and Valentine Zimny; and Ręczniaks (manual laborers): Val. Kaczka, Fr. Gay, Jak. Kamin, and Jak. Kaczmarek. Also labeled is the orchard (Obstgarten), the edge of the lord's lake (der Herrschaftliche See[rand]), and outbuildings (Vorwerks). As translated by William F. Hoffman, the label reads:

> *This is the map of the border established between the lake shore belonging to the lord's estate and the peasant gardens at Groß Jeziory in Schroda county. According to the border established as a result of consolidation of the estate, prepared in May, 1852 by von Ziehle, Vorw[erk] Inspector.*

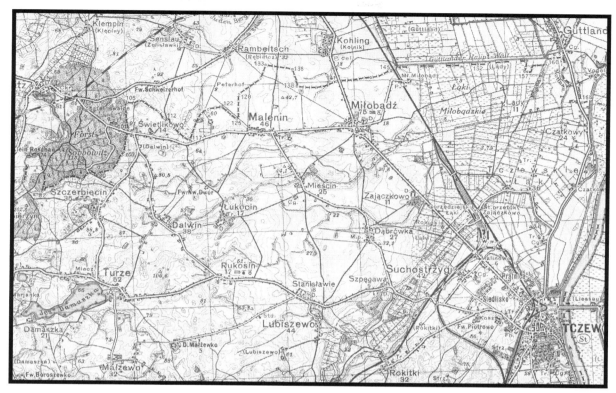

*This 1935 WIG map of Tczew (Dirschau) is available online from **http://mapywig.org**.*
The map is P32-S27 TCZEW and the color-coded map's scale is : 1:100,000.

How do I find maps for pre-World War II?

The Wojskowy Instytut Geograficzny—WIG for short, and the name means Military Geographical Institute—is a treasure trove of information about pre-World War II Poland. During the period 1919-1939 it compiled and published maps and geographic materials that have been scanned and put online. The size of the files range from 15 to 22 megabytes. The Web site also hosts an interactive forum and a selection of articles from the period before World War II on both Polish and foreign cartography. The site includes a Polish-English map vocabulary list explaining, for instance, that Br. is an abbreviation for *browar*, "brewery." ***www.mapywig.org***

The map featured above is from the WIG Web site. A copy of the same map was received from the library of Congress, although in black and white. A notation on the back of the map reads: Polish Series, G 6520.S100. p6, sheet 32-27, 1935.

These maps, and other period maps for Europe, can be ordered free of charge via the Library of Congress "Ask the Librarian" program. Access the page using the **Geography & Map** tab under **Special Formats and Genre**. Be as specific as possible and try to identify the village by name (Polish and German if necessary) and by longitude and latitude. Caution: if you request the maps via the Cartography Web site you will be charged a fee. Do not forget

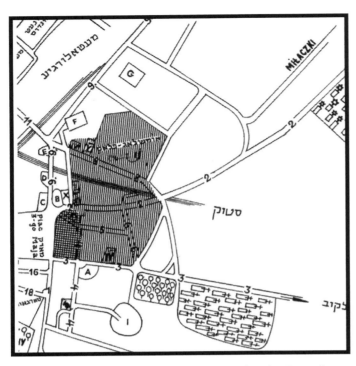

Map of Nova Rodomsk now known as Radomsko. From the Radomsko Yizkor book, 1967. Courtesy of Marilyn Brenner.

to request the key or legend for the map to interpret the symbols. *www.loc.gov./rr/askalib*

Accessing Yizkor Books: Yizkor (Memorial) Books are some of the best sources for learning about Jewish communities in Poland. Groups of former residents, or *landsmanshaftn*, have published these books as a tribute to their former homes and the people who were murdered during the Holocaust. *legacy.www.nypl.org/research/ chss/jws/yizkorbookonline.cfm*

Barry Hantman returned to Poland using his family's Yizkor book to find a cemetery. The following excerpts are from his story:

> *The map we had brought was completely useless. That's to be expected when you attempt to use a 75 year old map which had been copied from a Yizkor book as your street map. The map is 90% in Yiddish which makes it impossible for anyone living there today to make heads or tails of it. Rodomsko and its road system changed significantly in the intervening years. Even the street names shown in Polish have changed over the years. However, there were a few landmarks which helped to guide us. The major roads shown on the map still existed (under different names) and the plaza in the middle of town, shown on the map as 3-go Maja Plac2, still exists. There was a sign, one in the center of town, that shows a current map of the complete town. I was able to line up the old map that we had brought with the one on the sign and was surprised to find that the map on the sign showed a cemetery exactly where the 75 year old map showed the old Jewish cemetery. In fact, it was the only cemetery shown on the sign. The Christian cemetery shown on my 75 year old Yizkor Book map was not marked on this new map.*

For more information see: *www.hantman.net/geneology/LittmanStory/story.htm*

Chapter 6:

Record Keeping
and Handwriting in Poland

You do not need to be fluent in Polish, Russian, German, and Latin to successfully research records for your ancestors. What you do need is an overview of the history of the records, such as: birth, marriage, and death (BMD); an understanding of the rubrics common to Polish records; and techniques for deciphering hard to read handwriting or script. Three key online sources for further study include the FamilySearch, the State Archives of Poland, and an article entitled *Vital Records in Poland* by Warren Blatt. ***www.jewishgen.org/infofiles/polandv.html***

History of Sacramental and Vital Records in Poland

The ecumenical Council of Trent opened on 13 December 1545 and closed on 4 December 1563. Its main object was to define the doctrines of the Church in answer to the heresies of the Protestants. A further purpose was the execution of a thorough reform of the inner life of the Church by removing the numerous abuses that had developed. In 1547, the Council of Trent decreed that records be kept of the sacraments each person received and developed specific guidelines on record keeping—the rubrics. The red ocher headings in a record book were called rubrics and soon the rules to conduct liturgical services or maintain sacramental records took on the term as well. Each Polish partition had a separate time line for record keeping. Beginning in 1782, parish priests also kept registers of non-Christians; so, entries concerning Jews may be found in Catholic registries. Jewish BMD registers were also drawn up by officials—rabbis. In 1874, the keeping of BMD registers was entrusted to separate officials, so called registrars.

The contents of 19th and 20th century registers, both Catholic and Evangelical, were similar. The certificate of baptism may have included: the date of birth; details of the ceremony (where and when it was performed); particulars of the child's parents (Catholic records did not record the name of the father in the case of an illegitimate birth); the names and occupations of the godparents; and the priest administering the baptism. The certificate of marriage often included: the date of marriage; location of the ceremony; the priest solemnizing the ceremony; the couple's names and their social, marital, and legal status; and the names of their parents and the witnesses. The death certificate might have recorded: the date and place of death; age; name of the deceased; cause of death; marital status; particulars of the surviving spouse and orphaned children; the administering priest; and the date and place of the funeral. In the case of burial, many records briefly reference the churchyard; not a plot indicated by row and grave number. Term graves, the tradition of reusing graves, is a common practice in Poland, even today. The family is required to pay a leasing fee according to a schedule.

Church Registers

Data of a genealogical nature are included in records kept by parishes which include: parishioners, marriage banns, parish announcements, those participating in religious instruction at school, sodalities, and charities. Registers of religious orders may also be helpful for genealogical purposes.

Civil Records

The column format of record keeping was put into place in Galicia starting in the late 1700s with clerics doubling as a civil registrar. The object was to maintain accurate records for forced military conscription. Prior to 1874 in the Prussian sector, BMD registers were kept for each denomination by parishes; those of the Jewish faith—by municipal authorities. In 1874, public registry offices were established. They kept three types of registers: Births (A.), Marriages (B.), and Deaths (C.). Civil registration in the Russian partition began in 1804 under the Napoleonic Code. Written in narrative form, they were recorded in Polish. Russification was imposed as a result of the 1863 uprising. Although the language of the documents did not change until 1868, the format remained the same until 1918.

An introduction to genealogical materials held at the State Archives of Poland can be found online.

www.archiwa.gov.pl/lang-en/for-archive-users/genealogy/407-types-of-sources-used-for-genealogical-queries.html

Civil Registers
Birth (A.) and Death (C.) Records.
From the collection of Joseph F. Martin.

C.

Number *80*

Bnin on *6 August 1876*

Before the undersigned civil servant appeared today the individual known to me through *the person known to me*

the shoemaker, Thomas Nowacki

the day laborer, Maryanna Skibinska,

living in *Swiątniki*

and reported that *Franziska Skibinska,*

3 years old, *Catholic* religion,

living in *Swiątniki,*

born in *Psarski,*

daughter of the reporter born Frankowiak,

and her deceased husband Matheus Skibinski

from *Mieczewo*

in *Swiątniki* in the reporter's home

on the *fifth of August*

in the year one thousand eight hundred *seventy six forenoon*

at seven

passed away.

Read, approved and signed

Maryanna Skibinska

The civil servant

Müller

In agreement with the central registry

Bnin 6 on *August 1867*

The civil servant

Müller

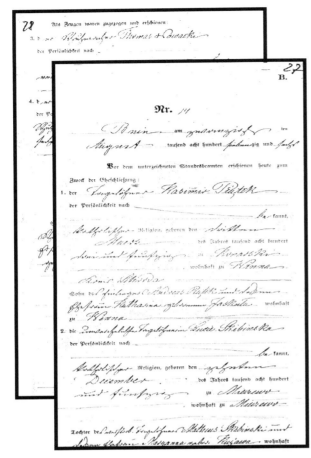

Civil Register
Marriage (B.) Record.
Page one of a two-page document.
From the collection of Joseph F. Martin.

Number *14*
Bnin on 20 August 1867

Before the undersigned civil servant appeared today for
the purpose of marriage
1. the *day laborer Kasimir Piątek*
the individual personally known to me
Catholic religion,
born the *third March* of the year
one thousand eight hundred *fifty three*
in *Konarski*
living in *Winna, Sroda County,*
son of the *small farmer Andreas Piątek*
and his wife Katharina, born Jaskuła,
living in Winna

2. the *unmarried day laborer Lucie Skibinska*
the person familiar to me
Catholic religion,
born the *tenth of December,*
one thousand eight hundred *fifty*
living in *Mieczewo,*
the daughter of the *deceased day laborer Matheus Skibinski*
and his wife Maryanna, born Kujawa,
living in *Mieczewo*

The first page of the marriage document is transcribed above: The following information is an abstraction of page two.

As witnesses had come and were present, 3. the shoemaker Thomas Nowacki the individual
known to me nine and forty years old living in Bnin 4. the day laborer Joseph Strugarek the person
familiar to me through the person known to me the shoemaker Thomas Nowacki six and thirty
years old living in Radzewo. In the presence of the witnesses the civil servant asked the engaged
individually and after each other the question: whether they would declare that they would enter
matrimony with each other. The betrothed answered this question affirmatively and followed the
statement of the civil official that he now by the power of the law declared them legally married.
Read to and approved and signed. Signed by crosses by Lucie Skibinska because of illiteracy.
Signed by the others Kazimierz Piątek, Jozef Strugarek, Thomas Nowacki, The civil servant
Müller In agreement with the central registry Bnin, 20th August 1876 The civil servant Müller

Polish BMD registers created prior to the end of the 18th century provide more information on the genealogy of noble and middle-class (bourgeois) families and less on peasant families. Entries for peasants only included given names and, occasionally, occupations. Specifically in Russian Poland, Jewish registrations are found in the Roman Catholic civil transcripts (1808-1825). Beginning in 1826, separate registers were kept for each religious community (Catholic, Jewish, Protestant, Russian Orthodox, Greek Orthodox, etc.). Blatt provides a timeline of important dates including:

1805—West Galicia: Jews required to take surnames—Austrian government mandate.

1821—Kingdom of Poland: Jews required to take surnames—Russian government mandate.

Noble Families

District and municipal registers can be used for genealogical queries on noble families. These records include the names of owners of estates and information on: family members, witnesses, debts and liabilities, dowries, and last wills. Information on noble and middle-class families may be found in mortgage registers of the 19th and 20th centuries. The registers provide information not only on subsequent owners of estates, buildings, and palaces in towns; but, also provide data on the heirs and their relationship to the deceased owner.

Are the records different for the 20th Century?

During the inter-war years (1919-1939), various provisions concerning the manner of keeping public registers were standardized by regulations of the Supreme Court. Under the decree of 25 November 1945, the registration of civil records was introduced throughout Poland and the new state Civil Records Office (Urząd Stanu Cywilnego a.k.a. USC) was formed. They keep public registry records and preserve them for a period of 100 years before transferring them to the state archives.

I can't read the Handwriting!

Genealogists are not the only researchers who need to study past and present handwriting styles. The American Society of Questioned Document Examiners (ASQDE) and the European Network of Forensic Handwriting Experts (ENFHEX) do this as well. Their goal is to detect counterfeit documents; our goal is to extract information from scribe written records, which at first glance, may seem indecipherable. As you study the handwriting, you may begin to actually read the information encoded in the vintage script. You may get to know the scribe by the unique characteristics of their handwriting—slant, size, shading, and letter forms—as no two individuals ever write exactly alike.

tu, te, ta-ta-ry, wa-ta, nu-ta, ru-ta, mo-ne-ta,
li-te-ra, mo-ty-le, to-wa-ry, mi-łe la-to, ta-la-ry.

b = b - b

ba, be, ob, bu-ba, ba-ba-ba, ro-bo-ta.

bo, bi, bo-bu, ba-ry, ba-ra-ny, bo-ro-wy, ba-
ty, ra-na bo-li, o-ni bi-li ba-ta-mi ba-ra-na.

h = h - h

hi, ho, hu, hu-la, ha-le.

ha, ho, hu-ra, hu-ba, ha-le, ho-ło-ta, ha-li-na,
hu-la-my, o-ni ha-mo-wa-li.

k = k - k

*ka, ku-ba, ko-ło, oko, oko-wy,
ko-ni-ki*

ka-wa, ra-ki, ha-ki, ko-ra, ku-ła-ki, ko-ro-na,
bu-ra-ki, ko-wa-le ro-bi-li ha-ki.

koń ma ko-py-ta, je-leń ży-je w le-sie, słoń
jest du-ży, słoń-ce świe-ci jas-no, nie-mow-lę
ma ma-łą dłoń, ja-błoń roś-nie ko-ło pło-tu,
ość, kość, złość, waśń, pleśń, bo-jaźń.

ch = ch - ch

cha-ta, u-cho, głu-chy, ko-żuch

cho-ro-ba, chleb, słuch, węch, i-dę su-chą u-li-
cą, bez o-cho-ty nie-ma ro-bo-ty, za-pach
kwiat-ka jest mi-ły, go-łę-bie gru-cha-ją, słu-
cha-my śpie-wu sło-wi-ka, mam słuch, wzrok
i węch, da-chy do-mów kry-ją bla-chą.

sch = sz - sz

szu-ba, mysz, du-sza, ma-szy-na

szy-ba, szy-ja, ka-sza, ko-szu-la, szal, szał,
szum, kosz, pi-szę pió-rem na ze-szy-cie, mysz
je sło-ni-nę, scho-waj flasz-kę do ko-sza, szewc
ro-bi bu-ty ze skó-ry, u-szy-ma sły-szę każ-dy
sze-lest, szy-by są ze szkła, sza-nuj-my i słu-
chaj-my star-szych.

t T f F z Z

*Tomasz, Feliks i Zofja ko-
chają rodziców.*

Tadeusz Kościuszko pobił Moskali pod Racła-
wicami. Tatry, to najwyższe polskie góry.
Jan Sobieski gromił Turków i Tatarów pod
Lwowem, Żurawnem i Wiedniem. Na Śląsku
jest miasto Zabrze i wieś Zaborze.

u U y Y x X

*Ubóstwo jest następstwem
lenistwa*

Uszu mam dwoje. Utrzymuję je czysto. Zna-
ki X i Y są literami. Używa się ich rzadko.
Imię Xawery czyta się tak: Ksawery.

o O c C g G

*Onufry i Cyryl są kupcami.
Oni mieszkają w Gnieźnie*

Odra jest dużą rzeką. Grzegorz pojechał do
Częstochowy. Ojczyzna nasza rozciągała się
od Gdańska po morze Czarne.

l L ł Ł s S

*Las jest wielki i cienisty.
Łatwo w nim zabłądzić
Sowa lata nocą.*

Władysław Łokietek odzyskał walecznie tron
polski. Lwów jest stolicą Galicji. Święty
Stanisław Szczepanowski był biskupem kra-
kowskim.

Copybooks

The handwriting experts maintain collections of copybooks from a range of countries and time periods. It allows them to compare the possible forgeries using authentic handwriting styles. To put it into context, you used a copy book or primer when you learned to read and write. The Spencerian Method was taught in American schools until the mid-1920s, followed by the Zaner-Bloser Script and the Palmer Method. Two recent articles in the American press entitled *Cursive, that's so Last Century* and *Schools Adjust How Writing is Taught in Text Age* forecast the use of 20th century copy books by 21st century genealogists to decipher the written word. Just as the evolution of handwriting was influenced by early technology—they wrote longer sentences because they did not want to lift up the pen and dip it in ink again—the texting generation prints rather than writes and rarely uses longhand, reserving it for their signatures. Libraries and online sites offer us access to copybooks used in the 19th and 20th centuries.

Polish Primers

The examples at left are from the Digital Library of Zielona Góra and the Polish primer *Elementarz Polski z Czytanką do Użytku Jeńców* (*ABCs of Reading for the use of Polish Prisoners*) published in 1918. They offer a nice comparison between the German black font that was popular in the German and Austrian partitions, in comparison to cursive and manuscript examples of the same letters as used in Polish documents. Phonetic combinations are illustrated showing how the *sz* in Polish is represented as *sch* in German. The page with lined paper shows the Polish method of writing the letter z without a descending loop. Page 25 of the primer offers a good illustration of the formation of the letters C, G, L, Ł, and S; all of these letters are hard for the Palmer trained writers to decipher. Additional books on the site include the primer *Elementarz, czyli początkowa nauka czytania i pisania* which offers practice guides throughout the book complete with the Polish diacritical marks. They include the kreska (ć, ń, ó, ś, ź), the kropka (ż), the ogonek (ą, ę), and the stroke (ł). When searching for primers in the digital library, use the Polish word for elementary: Elementarz. Why not print out the practice pages with the italicized grid and try to duplicate the form of the letters? *www.zbc.uz.zgora.pl*

Translation Aids

Now that you have trained your eyes to recognize old styles of handwriting, it is time to build your vocabulary of religious and secular terms found in the records. A contemporary Polish-English dictionary will not be very helpful with the records from the 1800s. There are several tutorials online that help researchers become acquainted with the words and symbols used and the nuances of record keeping. I do not have a background in foreign linguistics and I had to become familiar with the languages in which my ancestral records were written. I was able to accomplish my goals by studying the Word Lists created by the FHL. They offer research guidance on their Web site for fifteen different languages. An excerpt from the Latin, Polish, and German Word Lists follows, as well as the introduction of their Russian Word List, which is currently in draft form. ***www.familysearch.org***

Latin is the mother language for many modern European languages. Many words in English, Spanish, French, and other languages resemble Latin words and have the same or similar meanings. Latin was used in the records of most European countries and in the Roman Catholic records of the United States and Canada. Because Latin was used in so many countries, local usage varied. Certain terms were commonly used in some countries but not in others. In addition, the Latin used in British records has more abbreviations than the Latin used in European records.

Polish is a Slavic language related to Russian and Czech. It is used in genealogical sources throughout Poland. Before 1918, Polish-speaking territories were divided between Russia, Germany, and Austria. Records written before 1918 may be in German, Russian, Latin, or Polish. In Russian Poland, Polish was the official language for vital records from 1808 to 1868. From 1868 to 1917, Russian was the official language. In German Poland, most records were kept in German or Latin, though some were kept in Polish. In Austrian Poland, most records were kept in Latin. Some records were kept in German and some in Polish. Polish is also used in the records kept in some Polish communities in the United States.

German is spoken in Germany, Switzerland, and Austria. Records written in German may be found in these countries and also in parts of Poland, Denmark, Luxembourg, Czech Republic, Hungary, and wherever German people settled. There are several different dialects in the German language. For example, in the province of Westphalia and other areas of Germany that border the Netherlands, you may notice words that are closely related to Dutch words. You may find the Dutch word list useful when working with these records. In addition, German is found in some early records of the United States, such as in Pennsylvania, Texas, Wisconsin, and other states where Germans lived.

Russian is a Slavic language. The Slavic languages are divided into three groups. Russian, Belorussian, and Ukrainian are East Slavic languages. The West Slavic languages are Polish, Czech, and Slovak. The South Slavic languages include Bulgarian, Serbo-Croatian, Slovenian, and Macedonian. Russian is the language of the Russian Republic, and was the official language of the Soviet Union. It was also used in official records in parts of Poland, Finland, and Alaska.

Here are the steps to finding these informative Word Lists. Under **Start Your Family**

History, select **guides**. Then under **Document Types**, choose **Word List** to decide which of the 15 options of **Genealogical Word List** would be helpful in your research.

Are there sample translations of Polish Napoleonic Records online?

The Society for German Genealogy in Eastern Europe hosts Jack Bowman's Polish Translation Aids. The SGGEE site contains pages of Polish language Napoleonic records. Bowman cleverly assembled a page for each of his examples showing the actual handwritten document with the typewritten words below, in both the original language and the English translation. The Web site also offers *Quick Jumps* which are links to extremely helpful sources such as: *Alternate Given & Surnames; Books; Dictionaries & Translators; German Occupations; German Script; Non-English Fonts; Sample Translations—Polish;* and *Sample Translations—Russian.* **www.sggee.org/research/translation_aids**

How do I read an old German document?

The Immigrant Ancestors Project (IAP), sponsored by the Center for Family History and Genealogy at Brigham Young University, offers Script Tutorials for reading old handwriting and documents. The languages covered include English, German, Dutch, Italian, French, Spanish, and Portuguese. The tutorials were designed to prepare volunteers to extract accurate information from records for IAP. The project's focus is on European records of emigration.

Many documents in the German and Austrian partitions of Poland during the 18th and 19th centuries were handwritten and kept in the German language; therefore, a tutorial in this script can unlock needed information. The key is learning to read old German by developing the ability to write it yourself. By the time you finish their learning exercises, they say, you will be able to write words, sentences, and phrases in both Gothic and Fraktur style. These skills will make it easier for you to use German gazetteers and read German documents. The site is divided into four sections: **Getting Started, Handwriting & Typefaces, Extraction Guidelines**, and **Transcription Tests**. *www.script.byu.edu/german/en/welcome.aspx*

A SAMPLER of DATES and TIMES of DAY in FIVE LANGUAGES				
ENGLISH	**POLISH**	**LATIN**	**GERMAN**	**RUSSIAN**
MONTH				
January	styczeń	Januarius	Januar	январь
February	luty	Februarius	Februar	февраль
March	marzec	Martius	März	март
April	kwiecień	Aprilis	April	апрель
May	maj	Maius	Mai	май
June	czerwiec	Junius	Juni	июнь
July	lipiec	Julius	Juli	июль
August	sierpień	Augustus	August	август
September	wrzesień, VIIber	September, 7ber, VIIber	September, 7ber, 7bris	сентябрь
October	październik, 8ber, VIIIber	October, 8ber, VIIIber	Oktober, 8ber , 8bris	октябрь
November	listopad , 9ber, IXber	November, 9ber, IXber	November, 9ber, 9bris	ноябрь
December	grudzień, 10ber, Xber	December, 10ber, Xber	Dezember,10ber, 10bris, Xber, Xbris	декабрь
DAYS OF THE WEEK				
Sunday	niedziela	dies Solis	Sonntag	воскресенье
Monday	poniedzłek	dies Lunae	Montag	понедельник
Tuesday	wtorek	dies Martis	Dienstag	вторник
Wednesday	środa	dies Mercurii	Mittwoch	среда
Thursday	czwartek	dies Jovis	Donnerstag	четверг
Friday	piątek	dies Veneris	Freitag	пятница
Saturday	sobota	dies Saturni	Samstag	суббота
TIMES OF THE DAY				
in the morning	rano/z rana	mane	morgens	утром
in the forenoon	przed południem	ante meridiem	vormittags	
at noon	południe/w południe	meridie	mittags	полдень
in the afternoon	popołudniu/ z południa	post meridiem	nachmittags	
in the evening	wieczorem/w wieczóra	vespere	abends	
at midnight	północna godzina	media nox	mitternachts	полночь
hour	godzina	hora	Stunde	час
early (A.M.)	pred południem	ante meridiem	früh	анте Меридия
late (P.M.)	po południn	post meridiem	spät	Меридиа пост

A SAMPLER of GENEALOGICAL WORDS in FIVE LANGUAGES				
ENGLISH	**POLISH**	**LATIN**	**GERMAN**	**RUSSIAN**
birth	urodzin	partus	Geburt	рождение
burial	pogrzeb, sepultura	nativitas	Begräbnis	похороны
Catholic	katolicki	catholicus	katholisch	католический
child	dziecię	infans	Kind	ребёнок
christening	chrzest	baptismus	Taufe	крещение
civil registry	Urzad Stanu Cywilnego		Standesamt	
confirmation	konfirmacja		Konfirmationen	
death	śmierć, zmarł,	defunctus	Tod	мертвая голова, смерть
father	ojciec	pater	Vater	отец, папа
husband	mąż	maritus	Mann	муж, супруг
index	spis, indeks	index	Verzeichnis	индекс
Jewish	żydowski	judaicus	jüdisch	еврейский
marriage banns	zapowiedzi	banni	Aufgebote	
marriage	małżenstwo	copulatus	Heirat	брак
month	miesiąc	mensis	Monat	месяц
mother	matka	mater	Mutter	мать
given name,	imię	nomen	Vorname	имя
surname	nazwisko	cognomen	Zuname	фамилия
parents	rodzice	parentes	Eltern	родителе
parish	parafia	parochia	Pfarrei	прихо́д
Protestant	ewangelicki	acatholicus	evangelisch	протестантский
wife	żona	uxor	Frau	жена, супруг
year	rok	anno	Jahr	год

A SAMPLER of GIVEN NAMES in FIVE LANGUAGES				
ENGLISH	**POLISH**	**LATIN**	**GERMAN**	**RUSSIAN**
MALE				
Albert	Wojciech	Albertus	Albrecht	Альберт
Andrew	Andrzej	Andreas	Andreas	Андрей
Charles	Karol	Carolus	Karl	Карл
Casimir	Kazimierz	Casimirus	Kasimir	Казимир
Emilian	Emiljan	Aemilianusus	Emil	Эмилиан
Francis	Franciszek	Franciscus	Franz	Фрэнцишек
Jacob/James	Jakub	Jacobus	Jacob	Якоб
John	Jan	Joannes	Johannes	Ян
Lawrence	Wawrzyniec	Laurentius	Lorenz	Лаурентюс
Nicolas	Mikołaj	Nickolaus	Nikolaus	Николай
Paul	Paweł	Paulus	Paul	Павел
Peter	Piotr	Petrus	Peter	Петр
Philip	Filip	Phillipus	Philipp	Фипии
Simon	Szymon	Simon	Simon	Симон/Семён
Valentine	Walenty	Valentinus	Valentin	Валенм
FEMALE				
Agatha	Agata	Agatha	Agathe	Агафия
Agnes	Agnieszka	Agnes	Agnes	Агнэсса
Angela	Aniela	Angela	Angela	Ангела
Catharine	Katarzyna	Catharina	Katharina	Камерина
Dorothy	Dorota	Dorothea	Dorothea	Дорофея
Elizabeth	Elżbieta	Elisabeth	Elisabeth	Елизавема
Genevieve	Genowefa	Genovefa	Genoveva	Геновефа
Gundie	Kunegunda	Cunegundis	Kunigunde	Кунегунда
Hedwig/Hattie	Jadwiga	Hedvigis	Hedwig	Ядвига
Jane/Joan	Joanna	Joanna	Johanna	Иванна
Lucy	Łucja	Lucia	Lucia	Люция
Laocadia/Lottie	Leokadia	Laocadia	Leocadia	Леокадия
Margaret	Małgorzata	Margareta	Margarete	Маргарима
Pelagia/Pearl	Pelagia	Pelagia	Pelagia	Пелагея
Valerie	Waleria	Valeria	Valerie	Валерия
Stella	Stanisława	Stanislava	Stanislausa	Станислав

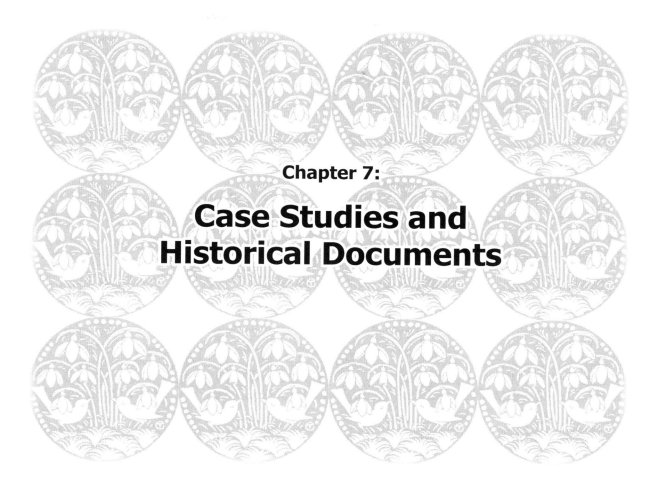

Chapter 7:

Case Studies and Historical Documents

Two of my most popular lectures are *Strategies for Locating Ancestral Villages* and *Behind the Scenes of the Polish Archives*. I have combined them in this chapter to demonstrate the research process and present a sampler of records. The lectures are based on case studies I have personally undertaken. I will present: documentation of primary records from microfilms; files located by Polish researchers; and summaries of trips to archives in a number of Polish cities that include the Auschwitz-Birkenau Memorial and State Museum and the Stutthof National Museum. As I met with each director I asked, *"Do you have unique genealogical materials that have not been filmed by the Church of Latter-day Saints?"* This open ended question was posed because I knew that LDS is most interested in microfilming birth, marriage, and death records; so, it was likely that the archives held other materials that could enrich a family historian's work. I advise researchers who are going to the archives to make sure to explore the online catalog before visiting.

I have prepared a number of case studies that include families from the Austrian, German, and Russian partitions of Poland; and the United States. Each starts with a summary of known information, followed by a problem and a plan to solve it. The case ends with a synopsis and suggestions where to find similar records for research.

It may surprise some readers to know that if the record books have been microfilmed, the film is what you will be accessing, not the actual records. This makes sense for the preservation of the record books. Use the available microfilmed records here in North America before you go to Poland. You want to make sure you are accessing unique materials while you are in your ancestral country. Poland's National Archives catalog is online and has links to all the regional archives throughout the country. *www.archiwa.gov.pl*

Check the archives Web site for the days and hours of access at each individual archive. Some close for a month in the summer. Many have a morning session, close for lunch, and end the day at 3 o'clock. The materials you are seeking will be in closed stacks and you will need to submit a request. Be sure to rank your requests in the order of importance because of possible time constraints. While many records are listed in the online catalog, there are additional materials that may be indexed in the finding aids at the individual archive. We North Americans are spoiled and want to have access to records like we do to burgers at the drive-in window—we want them now! We need to respect the Polish culture and go with an understanding that the copier may be locked away and only used by the director. My experiences have varied throughout Poland; but it is safe to say that you may have to return another day to get the copies you have ordered.

Case Study: Who was the rich man in the Adamski family lore?

The Adamski family did not have any paper records, only oral tradition. The family stories included the fact that they came from Poznań and they traveled in stages to the states, suggesting chain migration. The patriarch, Michał Adamski, was said to have worked in the gardens of a rich man, who also owned a large library and loaned books to him. The paper trail left by Michał's daughter, Mariana, who arrived in 1888, did not reveal any useful information in terms of an ancestral village. Many Poles gave a large city or the province instead of the village when asked for their place of birth. It was only when reviewing an old letter that my quest was pointed in the right direction. It read: *I know Uncle Jack's* [Jakub Adamski] *children were born in Poland.* This indicated that Jakub's family, who arrived in 1907, may have listed the name of the actual village when asked by the U.S. record keepers. (The questions asked of immigrants became more detailed beginning in 1906). Furthermore, Jakub's Polish born son, James, was the right age to have served in World War I and may have listed the village in his documents. Both hunches were correct in that the ship manifest and the citizenship he received when discharged from the army, listed the village of Rogalin. Additionally, the ships manifest listed Jakub's occupations as a coachman. A Google search for the village returned an article about a palace in Poznań. This was in fact the first clue that there was truth to the family story, because this was the palace of a rich Polish noble, Count Edward Raczyński. Further investigation revealed that the Count's ancestors had established the first Polish library in Poznań. Did Michał Adamski work in this Count's garden and was Michał's son, Jakub, Raczyński's coachman? Since parish registers documented the family in the area since 1690, I wondered if earlier generations also worked at the manor?

Will the archives have records about the Adamski family?

I made plans to travel to the Poznań archives and developed three goals for this first case study: one goal was to investigate the family lore that implied the Adamskis worked on a manor; the second was to see if Raczyński's records were available; and the third goal was to visit Raczyński's palace and estate in Rogalin. This was to prove in a sense the family story that my great-grandparents had met during the harvest.

My translator and guide at the State Archive in Poznań (Archiwum Państwowe w Poznaniu) was Kasia Grycza. As with all archives, whether in North America or Europe, there are certain procedures to follow. In this case, we registered at the office just outside the reading room and left our belongings in lockers. We filled out request slips for the books we were interested in. At the time of our visit, requests were limited to six books. Being aware that one volume may only hold a year of records, or as many as ten, we prioritized our requests. We returned in the afternoon when the ledgers were available. It is interesting that the records are kept in another building; and when it is raining, the 300 year old books arrive in a "granny" shopping cart with a plastic flap pulled over them for protection. The civil archives did in fact hold ledgers for the manor and the estate's accounting books. Would I be able to prove the story that Michał Adamski had worked for a rich man? I was interested in searching the relationship between the manor owners and the peasants who worked their fields.

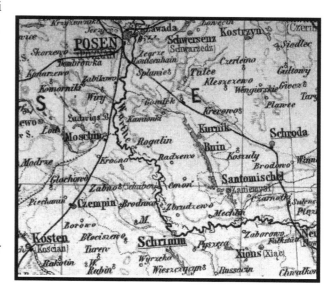

Before flying to Poland, I searched the archive's online catalogue and found an entry for budgets and accounts for the estate spanning 1848-1894. Once at the archive, we accessed the finding aid and identified additional ledgers of interest: *Inventory of Rogalin Farm 1759*; *Mortgage of Rogalin 1845*; *Bills and Budgets—Rogalin,*

Jezewo, and Korzkowo 1884-1895; Reports, Incomes, and Expenses from the Harvest 1891-1894; and *Kitchen Expenses 1775.*

What can be found in the budget books?

The 1889-1890 budget ledger listed the wages of the workers at the palace and the manor farm. The records were written in Polish and were divided by costs for the farm, forest, distillery, palace, garden, and retired people. Wages were recorded as a yearly amount in

German Marks as well as payments in wheat, rye, oats, peas, potatoes, salt, flax, sheep, wood, and cows. There was a column for an extra benefit for St. John's Night (*Noc Świętojańska*); but nothing was awarded to the workers in 1889-90. Michał Adamski was listed as working in the garden and received 60 Marks, 10 units of wheat, 3 units of rye, 2 units of oats, 2 units of peas, 12 units of potatoes, 2 units

of salt, and 1.5 units of flax. His son, Jakub, received a better wage of 750 Marks and more grains; but did not receive salt or flax.

Are there any other records regarding peasants?

The *Listy Duszy*, or List of Souls, were a civil record keeping device employed throughout Europe to keep track of the villagers who were required to register their household. These archived lists can be found in France, Italy, and of course, Poland. It was at the suggestion of the archivist in Poznań that we have a look at these records. While at first glance they seemed to be old notes, it was worth the experience to look through the scribble to read the data recorded about my ancestors. In this case, I found the Adamski family grouping as it was in the ancestral parish which was later duplicated in Michigan. It clarified that some of the marriages had actually taken place before they set sail.

The information for the List of Souls entry on the next page documents: house number; each inhabitant by name; occupation; date of birth; religion; marital status; village of birth; and kreis (county) of birth. An additional column recorded when they moved out of the village, and where they were going. In the entry for Wojtkowiak, he was listed as: a locksmith; married; Catholic; and born in 1863 in the village of Tulce, Kreis Schroda, Posen. It also indicated that he left the village on 1 January 1888 to come to America. Listed below his name were his wife, Mariana; and son, Jakub, who was born on 10 July 1887. I extracted the archive's list of villages included in the List of Souls collection and you will find it on the Sto Lat blog . *www.stolat-jensen.blogspot.com*

Does the manor still exist?

It was exciting to visit the estate of Count Edward Raczyński. His estate included the palace itself, and the manorial farm with many outbuildings. The manager, Mikołaj Pietraszak

Adamski descendants visit the miniature open-air museum scale model of historic structures in Poznań, including the Raczyński palace in Rogalin.

Dmowski, was just the right local person to meet to find out more about the estate. He had personally met the count, who lived to the age of 102. When the count died in London, it was Mikołaj's job to dismantle the exiled former Polish president's office and bring it back to the palace for display. Mikołaj put out a call to the region to find artifacts of the estate. The Raczyński Family Foundation now has a collection of black and white photographs, newspaper articles, and family recollections of what it was like to live and work on the Rogalin estate. As we took a tour of the grounds, he described a workday on the Prussian farm. Each morning, the workers needed to meet at the red brick gate precisely at 7 o'clock. There would be no work, and therefore, no wage for the late arrivals. The laborers on the farms would toil as a collective during the planting and harvest seasons moving from one village to the next. Dmowski suggested reading Raczyński's book, *Rogalin i jego mieszkancy,* which is the count's memoir about Rogalin and its inhabitants. The count describes his coach driver, Jakub Adamski, on page 47. Mikołaj also pointed out several paintings in the count's art gallery. I was particularly moved by Jacek Malczewski's *W tumanie* (In the Dust Storm) painted 1893-1894. This image is of a cholera epidemic sweeping through the field on the estate. Cholera and typhoid often swept through the villages with some families losing many children in a few weeks. Occasionally, the priest would make notations in the death records charting the course of the plague.

Manor records can be found throughout the continent as this was the economic structure of medieval Europe. Village descriptions provided by the *Słownik Geograficzny Królestwa Polskiego* can aid in identifying the manor owners in your area of Poland. There is also a map set that is available through the FHL in Salt Lake City that cross references manors and their owners in the Prussian partition. The set includes bound books and large color-coded maps. The *Historisch-Geographischer Atlas des Preußenlandes* was compiled by Hans and Gertrude Mortensen and Reinhard Wenskus. To find out more about manors and their owners, check the Web site *Central and Eastern European Magnates and Their Archives.* ***www.avotaynu.com/magnates.htm***

We set a day aside to visit the manors once owned by the Raczyńskis. The entire route covered approximately 16 miles. We visited the manor of Mechlin which is now a bed and breakfast. We mentioned to the owner that the kitchen ledger from 1778 listed their fish as far more expensive than the neighboring farms. He laughed and said, *"We still have the best!"* Further down the road we stopped at the village of Zaniemyśl. This community has a small island that Count Edward Raczyński (1786-1845) used as his retreat. When he was in residence, he would often have his workers sail on the lake and reenact British military battles. In Witold Molik's book, *Edward Raczyński,* there is an illustration featuring the mock battles. No longer a noble reserve, vacationers can camp on the island. Reenactors continue the battles "Zaniemyskie bitwy morskie" each July. ***www.wyspaedwarda.jms.pl/wypoczni.htm***

Case Study: What types of local resources are available in the region?

Many families begin their genealogy with family stories and possibly a document or two carried from the old world to the new. The Wendt family research began with three documents created in West Prussia in the 1880s. The first document indicated that Franz Wendt was the son of Paulina Stelmach

and Franz Wendt. It further stated that he was born in the village of Mühlbanz, Dirschau on 9 April 1869. The document was signed in 1889, which was the year Franz (b. 1869) came to the United States. The other family documents were created for his brother and his father in 1892. That was the year Franz (b. 1837), his wife Paulina, daughter Juliana, and younger son Adolph came to the United States. These documents helped to find the ship manifests; but the manifests did not aid in determining the correct home village of the Wendts. The certificates had a seal on them reading Mühlbanz; but it could not be located on a current map. After using the online gazetteer *Kartenmeister,* the village was pinpointed. The family did not hail from Danzig (Gdańsk) as stated on the Baltimore manifest; but further south, near the city of Dirschau (Tczew). This region of West Prussia was a mixture of Slavic and Germanic families living in harmony. A typical page in the Catholic parish registry shows the mix of surnames: Engler and Reschke; Jankowski and Wilmowicz. Working within these records, researchers move between Latin and German. The family was documented in the parish books as early as the 1700s. All the data was on microfilm enabling me to begin the initial research here in the states.

Jubilee Books

The second part of this case study entails visits to the ancestral villages in Poland. Polish researcher and guide, Kasia Grycza, prepared our schedule. We were going to meet Krzysztof Kowalkowski, a local author I met over the Internet. An engineer by trade, he is a regional historian by avocation. He writes books about villages and parishes, having published one on Miłobądz to commemorate the 750th anniversary of the parish founded in 1250. *www.krzysztofkowalkowski.pl*

Similar to parish jubilee books here in the United States issued to celebrate significant anniversaries, Kowalkowski's book chronicles far more years. While written in Polish, I was able to pick out my great-uncle's name and saw a photo in the book which included the mayor of the village, Roman Wendt. I mentioned this in an email to Krzysztof. Unaware he was going to take matters into his own hands, Krzysztof contacted the local newspaper before our arrival and announced that I would be doing research on the Wendt family. He arranged

  for extended family, including Roman, to arrive at the hotel to greet me and I was delighted to find that they brought family photos, documents, and pedigree charts. While I was not able to find a connection to their family during the meeting, upon returning home, I found our link was Piotr Wendt. I thought we were related even before I did the research because of the similar features between my great-grandfather, Franz, and Roman's ancestor Franciszek Wendt (1924-2002). It was eerie! During the reunion, Kasia demonstrated her skill at being able to translate from Polish to English and back again. Because of this, as I reminisce about the visit, I feel that I communicated directly with my cousins.

Parish Visits

Kasia arranged in advance the visit to the parish of Macierzyństwa NMP (Motherhood of the Blessed Virgin). This is the parish the Wendt family belonged to before coming to the United States. We had to plan around the priest's schedule. We were on the historic border between the free state of Danzig and Poland. The village of Miłobądz witnessed the German invasion on 1 September 1939. The church still bears the marks of the gunfire. Not far from the parish school, there is a monument in honor of a student that was killed on that day. This area witnessed much strife over the years, including Napoleon's 1806 campaign. Additionally, when the Treaty of Versailles set new boundaries after World War I, the division crossed directly through the community *"a line to be fixed on the ground passing between Mühlbanz on the south and Rambeltsch on the north."*

We proceeded to the Wendt family's earlier parish in Lubiszewo, Świętej Trójcy (Holy Trinity), where the family worshipped in the mid-1700s. We were warmly greeted by the priest's brother, who was also the sexton of the church. Even though the parishioners were preparing for First Holy Communion services, with the housekeeper busy ironing altar linens on the church floor, the sexton found time to show us the Madonna shrine embellished with coral, amber, and gold offerings.

State Archives in Gdańsk

As we continued our itinerary, we made our way to the State Archives in Gdańsk. Upon entering the hallway, we noticed an exhibit on display. Much to my delight, there was an etching from the 1600s of the church in Lubiszewo. I took this as a omen of the successful research to come. Stanisław Flis, the Assistant Director of the archives, pointed out additional materials of interest to genealogists. Using the finding aid in the reading room, we found a catalog for maps including a plan of a stable for the manor at Mühlbanz. The interview with Stanisław Flis can be found online. ***www.stolat-jensen.blogspot.com***

Kashubian Skansen

We also made a trip to the Open-Air Museum of Kashubian Culture in Szymbark, founded by Izydor Gulgowski and his wife, Teodora. It was the work of the skansen founders to document the heritage that began a renaissance for this ethnic group. Kashubs were some of the first Polish settlers in North America, including Detroit. I was intrigued by the culture and wanted to know more. They are a Slavic group, whose written language contains both Polish diacriticals and German umlauts reflecting the influence of their German neighbors. These outdoor museums are found throughout Poland and are an excellent way to experience the architecture and traditions of our forefathers.
www.cepr.pl

Read more about Kaszuby online.
www.pgsa.org

Stutthof concentration camp

The last stop on our journey involved the Stutthof Museum in Sztutowo. Krzysztof helped us select a case study for our visit to this museum archives. The museum is little talked about; and yet, it was the first Nazi concentration camp opened and the last to be closed. The camp was planned before the 1939 invasion to incarcerate priests, journalists, politicians, teachers—anyone who could lead the Polish resistance. I first read about the camp in *The Vanished Kingdom: Travels Through the History of Prussia* by James Charles Roy. While the book is from a German point of view, it led me to this historic site. So, our case study was for Józef Wiorek, a teacher from the village Alt Paleschken (Stare Polaszki). While we had an appointment with the archivist, she did not know whose file we would request. Within minutes she was able to retrieve a thick packet of information on Józef. Records show he had been in the camp hospital several times; most inmates were worked to death and did not survive as long as Józef. However, Nazi documents prove his life was ended when his heart was injected with phenol (carbolic acid). His wife, Zofia, had to pay for his death certificate, which inaccurately states the cause of death as weak heart and circulatory system.

Case Study Borderlands:
What happened to the records?

It was time to travel to the archives of Mława for this borderlands case study. On a previous trip to Poland, I sought out the place of birth of my grandfather, Anthony Przytulski. The first "shoe box" family record that led me back to a village in East Prussia was a document for Anthony's uncle, Mikołaj (Nicholas). Written in German, it stated that Mikołaj was the son of Johanna and Adam; and that he was born in Ciborz, Kreis Strassburg on 9 September

1865. The document above was dated 19 April 1888 in Lautenburg. Again, a gazetteer had to be used to be able to find out what the Polish name was for this community today. An earlier review of the microfilmed records at the FHC indicated that Nicholas was born in this East Prussian parish; but there were no entries for the rest of his family. Another document needed to be found that would give the geographic location.

Family lore said they moved from Germany to Poland. Anthony's documents caused some confusion. The older European handwriting on the 1896 Baltimore manifest made the village name look like "Gross Sense". His 1917 World War I draft registration recorded Cutsburg as his place of birth. His 1927 naturalization listed Płock as his last residence in Poland. When interviewed in 1977, he said he was born in Warsaw. It began to appear like he was born in Russian Poland, but where?

Sonya Nishimoto, Family History Reference Librarian, suggested the village was Groß Lensk, an East Prussian village now known as Wielki Łęck. Once the spelling was deciphered, over 200 years of records for the family were found; but not Anthony's! By using *Shtetlseeker* (see page 58), I was able to determine that Cutsburg was Kuczbork and

as fortune would have it, Anthony's records could be found at the archives in Mława. This family lived on the border between West Prussia, East Prussia, and Russian Poland. So, in the course of three generations the records for this family were found in three separate provinces all within a radius of about 22 miles. This is another reminder why genealogists tend to trust the data given closest to the event.

Case Study Russian Poland: Do Jewish Records still exist?

Returning home from the archives of Mława, I found that a patron at my local FHC had undertaken extensive research on his Jewish family from this area. Robert Tachna's Web site, *Tachna Family Web Album,* is in memory of his beloved family and includes background information on the surname and its religious roots. He includes Hebrew names, as well as Western names, in his ledgers. The family tree is based upon the descendents of Boruch Baer Tachna (born about 1730), the oldest known ancestor. Robert compiled the tree from many sources including records from the archives in Poland, FHC microfilms, and personal interviews. He has over 4,000 individuals and 1,000 unique surnames. His surname index begins with Abelson and ends with Zylbersztejn. It is interesting to see the records from Poland as they span the years 1822-1935 and show the change in both the

Tachna Family Web Album

language and style of record keeping in the city of Mława. Three translations from Tachna's site are provided. For more information check out his Web sites. ***www.tachna.com*** and ***www.zchor.org/tachna.htm***

19th of July this year, a remarkable monument in the renewed fenced Jewish cemetery of Mława. The monument which will be of 15 meter height and 8 meter width is made out of pillars, removed from a nearby site which was once a Nazi notorious military camp, called "NeuBerlin". The Nazis destroyed the Jewish cemetery of Mława, removing all the tombstones and making pillars of 1 x 1 meter to be installed in that camp. Now those pillars, made of Jewish matzevot, were removed back to the cemetery, and re-erected in this grand monument, in the shape of a huge "Menorah", on the hill where the Jewish cemetery was, facing the famous railroad of Gdansk-Warsaw.—Moshe Peles

1839 Marriage Of Ruchle Tachna & Zalman Wiegolowski

It happened in the city of Mława the thirteenth of December in the year 1839 at nine o'clock in the morning there personally arrived a Jew Wolka Lipshitz, a rabbi, with another Jew Zalman Wiegolowski, single and twenty years old, living in Mława. Both his parents are deceased and he states his interest with Ruchle Tachna, a single girl age twenty. Her father is deceased and her mother Dworja [Devorah] is living in the city of Mława . All the witnesses sign the paper. The religious ceremony of marriage between the couple happened in the city of Mława on twenty three November, the second and thirteenth of November, and the third day, seven of December in the year 1839. The marriage happened verbally by agreement between Abraham Wiegolowski, the father, Dworja Tachna the mother, and the newly married couple. They declare they made no agreement before the marriage. The marriage act was read and signed by the assistant rabbi.

1869 Birth of William D. Young

It happened in the town of Mława on the eighteenth of September, eighteen hundred and sixty nine at two o'clock in the afternoon. Hersz Jablon, tailor, discharged soldier, forty two years old, residing in the town of Mława, appeared personally in the presence of the witnesses, Zelman Niborski, fifty five years old, and Kalman Zachariasz Rozenman, fifty one years old, both of whom residing in the town of Mława, and presented us a child of male gender, testifying that it was born in the town of Mława on the tenth of September of the current year at twelve o'clock at night to his wife, the Jewess, Gitela Frymeta née Tachna, thirty years old. This child was given the name Wulf. This document was read to the testifier and the witnesses and signed by them.

As witnesses testifying about the death appeared

the synagogue sexton Józef Asz, age 55

the merchant Mendel Rotschild, age 50

Read, approved and signed

1917 Death of Izaak Jakub Tachna

Mława, April 16, 1917. Before the below undersigned official of the civil registry for religious matters of non-Christian belief appeared today the merchant Henoch [Chanoch son of Nutuh] Nutkiewicz, age 37, residing in Mława and notified, that the house-owner Izaak [Yitzhak Yakov son of Yehudah Ha-Levy] Tachna, age eighty six, of Jewish belief, residing in Mława, born in Mława to unknown parents, died in Mława on the twenty ninth of March, nineteen hundred and seventeen, in the afternoon at four o'clock. The notifier was related to the deceased as his son-in-law.

Case Study Galicia: How do you find records for Austrian Poland?

This case study starts with dilemmas and questions with the ultimate goal to identify the nuclear family and ancestral village of Agata (Agnazka) Zdziebko Wendt (1872-1908).

1. What methodology would help to identify which of the ten villages named Zarzecze is the one the Zdziebko family hailed?

2. The American documentation is conflicting and insufficient to support the hypothesis that Tomasz (Thomas) Zdziebko was the brother of Agata Zdziebko and her sister, Maria.

3. Was Agata Zdziebko's father Joseph Zdziebko?

4. Are there Austrian military records that can be searched?

The Zdziebko (a.k.a. Jepko) families emigrated to Michigan from Galicia around 1875-1890. Family letters refer to Thomas Zdziebko as a likely brother or half brother of Agata and Maria Zdziebko. Because Thomas' known residence was 169 Rich Street (about 1891-1918), the hypothesis is that Thomas was the first member of the family to come to America.

Zarzecze

It was a long process to identify the ancestral village for the Zdziebko family. The family members traveled at a time that was not in the traditional indexes for microfilmed records. It was not until the Ellis Island database and indexed Hamburg List became available that the puzzle pieces started to come together. First, Agata's 1892 manifest was discovered; but her birthplace was only listed as Austria. When her sister, Maria, arrived in 1897 the manifest reflected Zarzeze, Österreich. And when Agata's niece, Zofia, arrived in 1899 the last residence provided was W. Zaryyce. Lenius' Galcian gazetteer did not list a village with any of these spellings; so, another strategy was developed—search by surname alone. This generated a list of nine exact matches, and passenger Paweł Zdziebko (a possible relative?), had the closest match to the other village spelling with Zarzecze, Galicy Province being listed. It proved to be a correct spelling for a village in Galicia. In fact, ten villages shared the name (see page 59). By the process of elimination, the Zarzecze village records that LDS had microfilmed were checked without success. So, while Paweł lived in Indiana, not Michigan, it seemed prudent to investigate his U.S. records. His naturalization records indicated his birthplace to be in the county (gmina) of Jasło. And although his death record stated Anthony as his father, Jasło was a viable clue. A Polish researcher was hired to go to the parish to search the sacramental records. Success!

This part of the case study cannot end without sharing the difficulty in finding the 1880 manifest of the Tomasz Zdziebko family. The surname was misspelled (Edzielski) when it was extracted into the Ancestry database. When the first letter of the surname is incorrect, other methods need to be employed to find the record. In this instance, I searched by using Tomasz and Thomas, his country of birth as Austria or Galicia, and the year of birth and arrival plus or minus five. Frustrated historians can correct Ancestry's database by using **View/Add Alternate Info** found under **Page Tools**. The site will display the correction and who provided it.

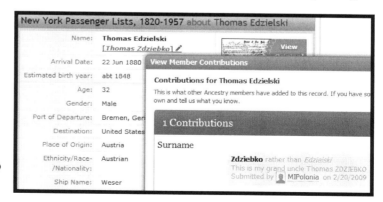

Family

The family was from the village of Zarzecze, in the parish of Dębowiec, located in the county of Jasło and the Austrian partition of Galicia. Sisters, Maria and Agata, and half brother, Tomasz, came to Detroit, Michigan. Their brother Antoni's son, Paweł Zdziebko, settled in East Chicago, Indiana. The hired Polish researcher worked with the parish records to find Agata's birth entry; and additional birth, marriage, and death records for the extended family. Tomasz, Maria, and Agata shared the same father, Jan Zdziebko; but different mothers. Tomasz was the son of Zofia Konopka; Katarzyna Szklarz was the birth mother of Maria and Agata. Along with the baptismal, marriage, and death records, a listing of the family living at house 91 was found in the parish office. The entry translates names and dates to read: Joannes

(Jan) 25 December 1822 in Maniów; Sophia (Zofia) 1831; Tomasz 9 December 1848; Marianna 12 January 1851; Antonius 21 May 1853; Katarzyna 1856; Paweł 27 June 1858; Wojciech 7 January 1861-12 May 1863. A later enumeration was found for house 91, listing a second Katarzyna born 1831; daughter Katarzyna 1856-1948; Maria 19 February 1869; Wiktorya 1 September 1870-1927; Agnazka 26 December 1872. Also living in the house was Jan and Zofia's daughter, Maria, her husband Alojzy Popp, and their children Władysław, Apolonia, and Ludmiła. The births and deaths of three other children—Justina, Zofia, and Agnieszka—were also found. This set of records helped sort out the traveling companions: Agata traveled with cousin Apolonia Dąbrowska; Maria with Wiktoria Wilk; and Zofia with cousin Apolonia Popp.

The European death records had two compelling annotations. The death of the Zdziebkos' cousin, Jan Trzeciak, took place in Florence, Wisconsin. His 1908 death certificate indicated he was stabbed to death! I ordered a newspaper article written about his death from the Wisconsin Historical Society. He was stabbed by another Pole at a party where the beer was flowing. It confirmed that his sister and mother were still in Poland. He was only 23 and was described as 6' 2" with a magnificent physique. He had suffered a broken leg from a mining accident and was behind in his rent. The Polish community paid his landlord for back rent. The second interesting death entry in the Dębowiec records was for Paweł Zdziebko's death, who died in 1880 at the age of 22. It indicated he was in the military at the time of his death in Vienna. He would have served in the Austro-Hungarian Army. More records to search!

Military Records

There is a guide on the Web site *Polish Roots* which can aid researchers seeking the name of the regiment in which a soldier enlisted. This is critical to finding the muster and service record. I accessed the massive regimental military records collection of the War Archives in Vienna via the microfilms of the Family History Library. There are indexes for locating officers; but not for enlisted men. Soldiers were recruited and enlisted in specific geographical locations. *Polish Roots* has a useful tool which shows the locations of regiments stationed throughout the empire. Essential Recruitment Location charts are found in Alphons Wrede's *Geschichte der K. und K. Wehrmacht* (*History of the Austrian and Austro-Hungarian Armed Forces*). The charts show regimental recruiting area assignments over an extended period of time. Steven W. Blodgett's *Austrian Military Recruitment within Galicia* online article presents an expanded version of these charts. ***www.polishroots.com/Resources/austrian_recruit/tabid/204/Default.aspx***

Using these online charts as a reference, I looked to see what records were available for Jasło. I found microfilms listed in the FHL catalog for baptisms, marriages, and deaths of military personnel. I also checked the Militär-Stammrollen 1858-1901—Registers of male

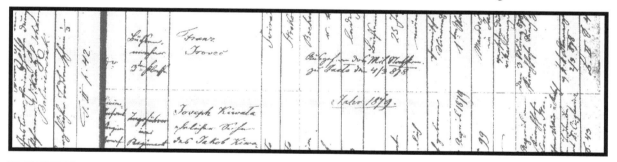

Friedhof Lorenz	Jaslower Friedhof (cemetery) funeral conducted by the priest Vikar HI. Johann Balwiercziak
	Official death record 1/3
	T.II p. 42
Infant. Regiment ? #40	Zugsfuhrer im Regiment Platoon leader
	Joseph Kiwala Legitimate son of Jakob Kiwala Platoon leader Wife: Marie born Stoj

births for military conscription, and the Kirchenbuch, 1822-1900 (baptisms, marriages, and deaths of military personnel). I did not find an entry for Paweł Zdziebko; but have included an entry (see page 91) for a fellow soldier from Jasło, Joseph Kiwała. He was the son of Jacob and died 24 April 1879. These microfilms can only be accessed at the FHL; so, on my next trip, I will double check the indexes and see if the villages south of Jasło, such as Dębowiec, were part of a different garrison. Another useful site is entitled *A Guide for Locating Military Records for the various Regions of the Austro-Hungarian Empire.* ***www.iabsi.com/gen/public/ahm.html***

Case Studies of World War II: Who are Displaced Persons (DPs)?

"We were all Displaced Persons, country-less refugees, who had lost our parents and grandparents, our families and our homes, our churches and our names, everything. It had all been left behind, buried in the great European grave yard that stretched from the English Channel to the Urals and from the Baltic Sea to the Mediterranean. And here we all were on this former troop ship, coming to start a new life in America. We could not have imagined what we would find and what we would become." —John Guzlowski

The Polish Mission Collection of World War II Museums

Walking on the historic Michigan campus of St. Mary's of Orchard Lake, edged by the fresh water lake, you are more likely to think of having a picnic than of the trauma of World War II. But here you will find museums commemorating the struggle and celebrating the survival of the Polish spirit during that war. The museums were created by the Polish veterans who came to Michigan as displaced persons, living their adult lives in Wayne, Oakland, and Macomb counties. The term Displaced Persons was coined during World War II and refers to millions of people removed from their native country as refugees, prisoners of war, or slave laborers. The majority were inmates of Nazi concentration camps or labor camps in Germany or Russia. As adults, they gathered together to document their story. Genealogy is important for these families, too. In the case of the Home Army and Air Force pilots, for example, the military heroes could not return home to Poland, because the Communist regime did not want any heroes. Many had been military officers exiled from the Kresy (eastern Poland), living on land they received after World War I for their military service. The families had a short history in the Kresy region having come from more western villages in Poland. Their children were born in DP camps during and after the war. A virtual museum is online. ***www.kresy-siberia.org***

The Polish Mission museums, each with a small archive and library, document: the Home Army; the Polish Army 2nd Corp; Polish Air Forces; the First Polish Armored Division; Polish Army Veterans in America; and the Association of Former Political Prisoners of German and Soviet Concentration Camps. These museums hold: survivor oral histories; art work; diaries; documents; photos; maps; uniforms; and related ephemera. The exhibits serve to document the war experiences of the Catholic Polish soldiers, families, and survivors. It also helps dispel the growing body of Holocaust revisionists' literature which includes denying the slaughter happened or refusing to call the camps by the proper term, Nazi Concentration Camps in Poland. The museums welcome everyone. Many people are unaware of the deaths of 3 million Polish Christians at the hands of the Nazi and Russian armies because this information was suppressed behind the Iron Curtain and during the Cold War. The museum collections transcend religion and speak of the struggle and suffering as well as the hope for freedom and liberation. On a 2009 research trip to Poland with Polish Mission Director, Marcin Chumiecki, we met with museum curators and archivists who are maintaining similar collections of camp art, survivor art, and autobiographies. *www.polishmission.com*

Children in Exile

The Polish community, under the leadership of the priests of Orchard Lake and the Felician Sisters of Detroit, welcomed war orphans to Michigan. Thirty-three boys, known as the Chłopcy z Polski and twenty-five girls referred to as the Girls from Colonia Santa Rosa,

Photo from the Archives of the Felician Sisters, Presentation of the Blessed Virgin Mary Province, Livonia, Michigan. In alphabetical order: Rozalia Bera, Teresa Bentkowski, Romualda Birecka, Kazimiera Brochocka, Maria Huk, Apolonia Jarząb, Władysława Karpowicz, Lidia Kolesnikowicz, Maria Kolesnikowicz, Nadzieja Kolesnikowicz, Wictoria Kowalska, Danuta Kuc, Kazimiera Kwiatkowska, Janina Lew, Maria Mazurczak, Irena Michalska, Wacława Michalska, Lucyna Mitura, Genowefa Mrozik, Łucja Pakiet, Antonina Pluto, Wanda Pluto, Janina Rajchel, Stefania Saraniecka, Leokadia Sedziuk.

Photo from the Central Archives of Polonia at the Orchard Lake Schools, Orchard Lake, Michigan. In alphabetical order: Kazimierz Baczyński, Józef Baniowski, Julian Baranowski, Kazimierz Bobrowski, Piotr Borkowski, Jan Andrzej Derecki, Marcin Dubis, Robert Glejf, Alfred Gołębiowski, Ryszard Goleniewski, Julian Jablonski, Zygmunt Jeziorski, Mieczysław Kaminski, Tadeusz Kamotowski, Tadeusz Kataj, Hilary Krolik, Mieczysław Kus, Kazimierz Kwiatkowski, Czesław Lichodziejewski, Józef Maksymow, Wacław Nagrocki, Stanisław Piekarski, Janusz Rękawek, Kazimierz Skowronski, Mieczysław Sukiennik, Franciszek Swastek, Bogusław Tubielewicz, Edward Wajda, Antoni Walawender, Zdzisław Witaszek, Stanisław Włodkowski, Józef Wolzynski.

Mexico arrived in Michigan as temporary students. But when their return to Poland at the close of the war became impossible, they became U. S. citizens and part of the fabric of the state of Michigan. These Polish children had their families torn apart and were sent to Siberia by the Russians at the start of the war. Their fathers were arrested and many killed like in the Katyn Forest Massacre. Their mothers were only given moments to gather a few things before they were all packed into cattle cars and sent on a month long ride to the Gulag—slave labor camps in Siberia. Making a long and tragic story short, those who lived were usually orphaned, and eventually made their way to various refugee camps including those in India.

Two groups were transported from Bombay to California in June and October of 1943 before being sent to yet another refugee camp in Santa Rosa, Mexico. The girls arrived in the United States via the *USS Hermitage* sailing from Bombay, India to San Pedro, California on 24 October 1943. They were taken to the Polish refugee camp of Santa Rosa in Leon, Mexico.

The boys, sponsored by SS Cyril and Methodius Seminary, left Calcutta and arrived in New York via the *USS General M. B. Stewart* on 24 November 1945. The manifest includes a margin note regarding the head tax payment made by the seminary. Antoni Walawender was aboard, and wrote about his experiences:

> *"My attempt to describe the nature of my survival in southern Kazakhstan would have been more graphically detailed, if I had kept a diary. I was too hungry, too exhausted, barely standing on my feet, always begging for food and shelter. Seeking a pencil, was not even on my mind."*

Many Polish communities in the U.S. also sponsored war orphans. A variety of records and related materials can be found in The National Archives in Washington D.C. See: *Records Relating to World War II Era Refugees. **www.archives.gov/research/ww2/refugees.html***

Case Study: Concentration Camps

There are three key stories the Polish Mission felt the need to validate: the oral history of Władysław Szcześniak; the provenance of Jan Komski's art work; and the legacy of an exhibit of Adam Grochowski's paintings.

Władysław Szcześniak (1911-1984)

The Polish Mission archives holds a 1982 recording of Władysław (Walter) Szcześniak detailing his incarceration at Auschwitz. He stated he was there when Father, now Saint, Maximillian Kolbe gave his life for another prisoner. Władysław's family had returned to Poland in 1916 when he was five years old. Like so many others who returned to Poland between World War I and World War II, they believed their dream had come true—they would live in a free Poland. Unfortunately, this was not the case. The concentration camps segregated the inmates who were born in America. There were many Americans, like Walter, in these camps. New databases are coming online documenting this segment of Polish history. Walter, an attorney by profession, is listed twice in the Auschwitz database:

> *Szcześniak, Ladislaus b.1911-02-04, camp serial number:18732,* and *Szcześniak, Władysław b. 4. 2. 1911 (Usdetham), camp serial number:18732, profession:prawnik*

If you are looking for relatives in the Auschwitz-Birkenau State Museum database, be sure to try the name in German and Polish and use Polish diacriticals. You can also search utilizing the place of birth. ***www.auschwitz.org.pl***

We wanted to authenticate Walter's story as an eyewitness to Fr. Kolbe's saintly acts. We had to find out when Walter arrived at the camp. We also wanted to document his birth in the United States, his stay at Auschwitz, and his return to the United States.

We first emailed the International Tracing Service (ITS) on behalf of Walter's niece since information is only given to the former prisoners or to their close relatives. They mailed copies of his records to her including his *A.E.F. DP Registration Record.* The information provided his: U.S. birth; residence in Warsaw; and transfer from Paris to Frankfurt confirming part of the oral history. Contact information for the ITS is provided. ***www.its-arolsen.org***

Office for Information on Former Prisoners

Registrations and Processing of Inquiries

Große Allee 5-9

34454 Bad Arolsen, Germany

trace.request@its-arolsen.org

Next, an email request was sent to the Auschwitz-Birkenau State Museum Archives with the following reply:

> *Archiwum PMAB - Auschwitz Museum Archives [archiwum@auschwitz.org.pl]*
> *T/D – 390 453I-Arch-i/ 3136/09*
> *In response to your request for information on Wladyslaw Szczesniak. I would like to inform your that in partially saved documentation of KL Auschwitz there is no information in which block he had been during this selection. In the testimonies by Jan Szegidewicz (named Sehid in the camp, number 16858) he mentioned that there were prisoners from the block no 14a, only. We have the following information about Wladyslaw Szczesniak (on the base of the Auschwitz files):*
> *Szczesniak Wladyslaw born February 4, 1911 in U.S. Detham, [sic] was brought to KL Auschwitz on July 25, 1941 from Krakow. He was registered as Polish political prisoner and received number 18732. Last mention in the files: January 29, 1944 – KL Auschwitz I, Block 21. There is no information about his further fate.*

The last search was in the New York ship manifests via Ancestry. Walter is documented in the New York Passenger Lists, 1820-1957. Walter Szczesniak arrived on the 23 March 1946 in the port of New York having sailed from the port of Le Havre aboard the *SS Gripsholm*. The header of the manifest is *List of United State Citizens*. Walter's U.S. address was listed as 4900 Oakland Street, East Dedham, Massachusetts and referenced his uncle, Frank Babcock.

We were able to substantiate Walter's oral history by documenting: his birth in the United States; his imprisonment and number in Auschwitz; and his DP records. Walter arrived on 15 May 1941 and was incarcerated there when Father Kolbe was taken to a camp cellar to die. After liberation on 3 May 1945, Walter went to France as a displaced person eventually returned to the United States.

Jan Komski (1915-2002)

The Polish Mission holds 12 pieces of art by Jan Komski; and we wanted to know more about the artist and the provenance of the collection. Komski was part of the first group of inmates to arrive at Auschwitz. Because he was a trained artist, he was assigned to the print shop and later an artists' studio, along with other professionally trained illustrators. The talented artists were forced to create art work for the Nazis in exchange for their survival. The gate at Auschwitz, which proclaims *Arbeit Macht Frei (Work makes [one] free)*, was created by a Catholic blacksmith, Jan Liwacz, camp number 1010. Early arrivals did not receive a tattoo on their forearms; but rather on their chests. Jan's work is important in that he shows the Catholic inmates alongside the Jewish prisoners. Komski's history was well known by the Auschwitz-Birkenau State Museum archivists and curators. In early 2001, Jan's widow donated 106 pieces of his work to the museum.

A Capo and his Troops, watercolor, 27" x 21".
Komski's note: A Capo (Always a criminal, most likely a German), and his troops.
Courtesy of the Polish Mission at the Orchard Lake Schools.

Using the Auschwitz-Birkenau prisoner database, we find Jan listed twice, once under his alias, *Johann Baras, born 1915-02-03, camp serial number:564*; and another with his baptismal name, *Jan Komski, born 1915-02-03*. The first entry has an icon next to it to identify the data was taken from the record book *Transports of Poles from Cracow and other localities in Southern Poland*. The second entry indicated he was transferred to Mauthausen concentration camp where he was liberated in May of 1945 when he returned to Poland.

The archives at Auschwitz was able to share his camp photographs, records, and a biography created by their art museum. He is also indexed in two of Ancestry's Military databases— *Germany: Flossenbürg Concentration Camp Records, 1938-1945* and *Germany: Dachau Concentration Camp Records, 1945*. We were able to identify a larger body of his work, interview his wife about the donations, and verify his arrival in the United States in 1951. He became an illustrator for the Washington Post.

Adam Grochowski (1924-1992)

"Don't ever be an artist," his paternal grandmother warned him, "it will never earn the price of your bread."—Adam Grant, Figure Master

Adam Grochowski, later known as Grant, spent his youth during one of the most terrible periods in human history. He is a quiet testament to his Roman Catholic faith and the restorative power of the creative spirit. Imprisoned at the age of 18, he was in two of the most infamous concentration camps—Auschwitz and Mauthausen. Then he lived for five years in

a DP camp in Regensburg, Germany. His unique figurative drawing skill saved his life. After the war, art provided Adam a way to erase some of the horrors he had experienced by utilizing the female figure as a symbol of life and rebirth. Adam came to Michigan as a DP and became one of the top artists for the 1950s craze—CraftMaster's *Paint-by-Numbers*. A fine artist in her own right, his wife Peggy loaned an exhibit of his work to the Polish Mission. Peggy had one request of the Polish Mission—locate Adam's U.S. sponsor. We found that his voyage was aboard the *USNS General R. M. Blatchford*. Adam's destination in Detroit was 12196 Waltham, the home of his sponsor, Bronisław Stachura. Our search for the Stachura family was unsuccessful until Bronisław's married daughter, Dana Barrett, volunteered at the Polish Mission. Among her memorabilia was an old envelope with the Waltham address. This chance encounter allowed us to introduce Dana to Grochowski's family.

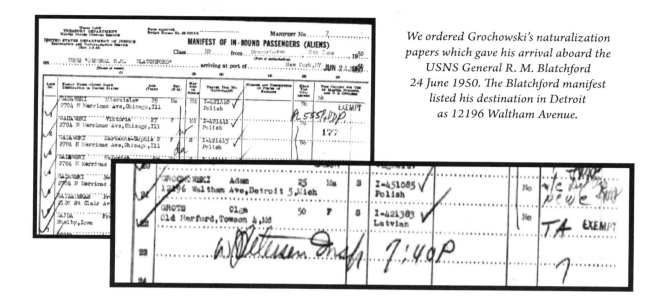

We ordered Grochowski's naturalization papers which gave his arrival aboard the USNS General R. M. Blatchford 24 June 1950. The Blatchford manifest listed his destination in Detroit as 12196 Waltham Avenue.

687	Kapsa	Edmont	13a Hohenfels Obpf Bavaria DP Camp	Stachura	Bronisław	12196 Waltham	1/7/1949
688	Kondijowski	Eugeniusz	39 Hohefels Bavaria DP Camp	Stachura	Bronisław	12196 Waltham	1/10/1949
689	Kondijowski	Eugieniusz	1300 Hohenfels Obpf, Bavaria DP Camp Germany	Stachura	Bronisław	12196 Waltham	1/7/1949
690	Ladendorf	Edward	Polish DP Camp Gablingen Flugplatz IRO Area 5 Augsburg, Germany	Stachura	Bronisław	12196 Waltham	1/3/1950
691	Ladendorf	Leonard	Polish DP Camp Gablingen Flugplatz IRO Area 5 Augsburg, Germany	Stachura	Bronisław	12196 Waltham	1/3/1950
692	Ladendorf	Rozalia	Polish DP Camp Gablingen Flugplatz IRO Area 5 Augsburg, Germany	Stachura	Bronisław	12196 Waltham	1/3/1950
693	Poprzecki	Karol	DP Camp Hohenfelds, Germany	Stachura	Bronisław	12196 Waltham	5/6/1949
694	Romaniuk	Jan	13a Hohenfels Obpf Bavaria DP Camp Germany	Stachura	Bronisław	12196 Waltham	1/7/1949
695	Romaniuk	Bronislawa	13a Hohenfels Obpf Bavaria DP Camp Germany	Stachura	Bronisław	12196 Waltham	1/7/1949
696	Sytek	Teodor	13b Altenstadt b/Schongau Upper DP Camp	Stachura	B. M.	12196 Waltham	3/30/1950
697	Sytek	Janina	13b Altenstadt b/Schongau Upper DP Camp	Stachura	B. M.	12196 Waltham	3/30/1950
698	Sytek	Franciszka	13b Altenstadt b/Schongau Upper DP Camp	Stachura	B. M.	12196 Waltham	3/30/1950
699	Wojciechowski	Nikodem	Rheine in Westphalen Danloup Kaserne DP Camp Germany	Stachura	Bronisław	12196 Waltham	12/2/1949
700	Wolna	Alicja	Polish DP Camp K.W.K. Amberg, Area 3 Germany	Stachura	Bronisław	12196 Waltham	10/21/1949
701	Wolny	Wilhelem	13a Hohenfels-Obvf Dreis Pasberg DP Camp Germany	Stachura		12196 Waltham	11/26/1948

The Polish Mission has a set of index card listing DPs and their sponsors.
Extracted into a spreadsheet format by Hal Learman, he was able to sort the sponsors by address.
It was Bronisław Stachura's address; and he had sponsored over 15 DPs.

DECLARATION OF INTENTION   No.
(Invalid for all purposes seven years after the date hereof)

Eastern Dist. of Mich   In the _____ District _____ Court

Southern Div.   ss: of United States at Detroit, Mich

(1) My full, true, and correct name is   ADAM MARIAN GROCHOWSKI

(2) My present place of residence is   4468 McDougall, Detroit, Mich

(3) My occupation is   stock man   (4) I am   26   years old. (5) I was born on   Oct 11, 1924

in Warsaw, Poland   (6) My personal description is as follows: Sex   male

color white complexion med., color of eyes blue, color of hair bro, height 6 feet 1 inches, weight 175 pounds,

visible distinctive marks   tattoo #156632 l. arm   race white, present nationality Polish

(7) I am not married;

Adam was naturalized on 22 August 1955 in Detroit, Wayne County, Michigan.
Adam's Declaration of Intention recorded "visible distinctive marks: tattoo #156632 l. arm."

Request for Genealogical Research — Prośba o badanie genealogiczne

Please print using capital letters or type all known information below.
Proszę napisać wszystkie informacje na maszynie lub drukowanymi literami.

1. **Surname, maiden name, and first name** (the exact name of the person being searched with variations.)
   Nazwisko, nazwisko panieńskie i imię (dokładne nazwisko poszukiwanej osoby i warianty pisowni):
   _____
   _____

2. **Religion** (please underline the applicable choice) – **Wyznanie** (proszę podkreślić właściwe):
   Roman Catholic   Greek Catholic   Evangelical   Jewish   Other _____
   rzymskokatolickie greckokatolickie protestanckie żydowskie inne _____

3. **Date** (as exact as possible; if the date is not known, give a range of 5 years).
   Data (możliwie dokładna; jeśli dokładna data nie jest znana, podaj w przybliżeniu do 5 lata).
   Year, month, day of – Rok, miesiąc, dzień: _____
   Birth – Urodzenia _____
   Marriage – Ślubu _____
   Death – Zgonu _____

4. **Place of** (exact name of town or village) – **Miejsce** (dokładna nazwa miasta lub wsi):
   Birth – Urodzenia _____
   Marriage – Ślubu _____
   Death – Zgonu _____
   Parish/Community – Parafia/Gmina _____
   County – Powiat _____
   Province – Województwo _____

5. **Photocopy of records requested – Prośba o kserokopię dokumentu:**
   yes or **no** (please underline the applicable choice – **tak** lub **nie** (proszę podkreślić właściwe)

6. **Other important information – Inne ważne informacje:**
   _____

   Information requested by – Prośba o informacje składana przez:
   Name and Surname – Imię i nazwisko _____
   Address – Adres: Street – Ulica _____
                       City – Miasto _____
                       State/Province – Stan/Prowincja _____
                       Zip/Post Code – Kod pocztowy _____
                       Country – Kraj _____

Jan Zdziebko	Zofia Konopka

Jan Zdziebko

P: Wojciech Zdziebko

& Marianna Laik

* 25.12.1822 Maniów by Szczucin

+ 09.08.1873 Zarzecze

Zofia Konopka

P Kacpra Konopki

& Wiktoria Masta

* 13.02.1831 Zarzecze

+ 11.03.1866 Zarzecze

marriage 23.11.1847 r. Debowiec

1. Tomasz   * 09.12.1848 Zarzecze   left for the USA

M. 1870's to Agata Skalba

2. Marianna   * 12.01. 1851 Zarzecze   + 28.03.1914 Zarzecze

M 16.09.1877 (Debowiec) to Alojzy Popp (Ostrawa-Moravia)

3. Antoni   *. 21.05.1853 Zarzecze   + no info

M 17.11.1875 (Debowiec) to Agnieszka Wietecha (Zarzecze)

4. Katarzyna   * 15.01.1856. Zarzecze   left for the USA

M 29. 05 .1881 (Debowiec) to Piotr Trzeciak (Zarzecze)

5. Paweł   * 27.06.1858 Zarzecze   + 05.12.1880 Vienna

(in the army)

6. Wojciech   * 07.01.1861 Zarzecze   + 12.03.1863 Zarzecze

7. Jakub   *. 17.06.1864 Zarzecze   zm. 04.01.1870 Zarzecze

- -

Jan Zdziebko

P: Wojciech Zdziebko

& Marianna Laik

*. 25.12.1822. Maniów by Szczucin

+. 09.08.1873 Zarzecze

Katarzyna Szklarz

p: Jan Szklarz

& Agata Bajoska

* 26.04.1831 Glinik Niemiecki

+ 11.02.1893 Zarzecze

M 28.05.1866 Debowiec

8. Marianna   * 03.01.1868 Zarzecze   + 03.01.1868 Zarzecze

9. Marianna   *. 19.02.1869 Zarzecze   left for the USA

10. Wiktoria   * 12.09.1870 Zarzecze   + . .1927 Stróże?

Stillborn girl * 12.05.1892 .   on the train to Cracow

11. Agnieszka   * 26.12.1872 Zarzecze   left for the USA

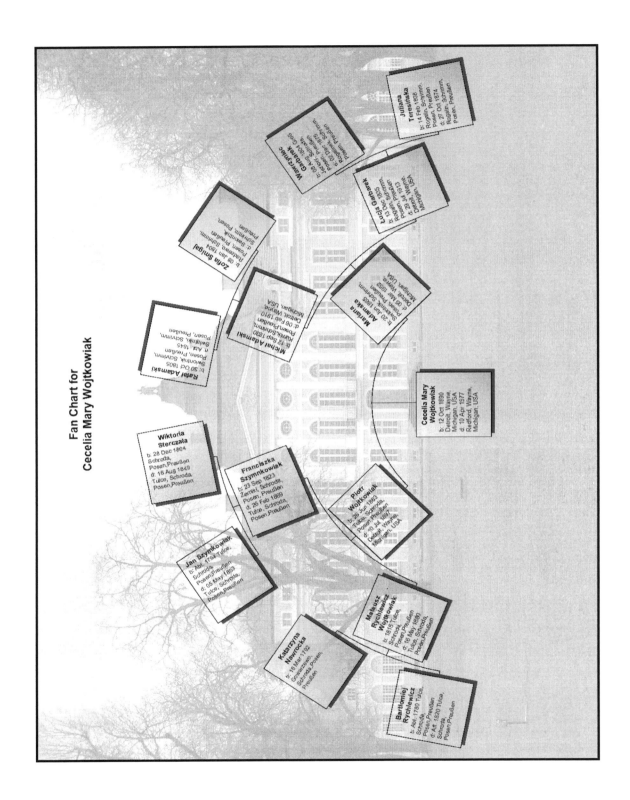

Fan Chart for
Cecelia Mary Wojtkowiak

Cecelia Mary Wojtkowiak
b: 12 Oct 1890
Detroit, Wayne,
Michigan, USA
d: 10 Apr 1977
Redford, Wayne,
Michigan, USA

Piotr Wojtkowiak
b: 29 Jun 1863
Tulce, Schroda,
Posen,Preußen
d: 10 Jul 1897
Detroit, Wayne,
Michigan, USA

Mariana Adamska
b: 20 Jun 1869
Schroda, Preußen
d: 05 Mar 1932
Detroit, Wayne,
Michigan, USA

Mateusz
Rychlewicz
Wojtkowiak
b: 1815 Tulce,
Schroda,
Posen,Preußen
d: 18 May 1890
Tulce, Schroda,
Posen,Preußen

Franciszka
Szymnkowiak
b: 23 Sep 1823
Zerniki, Schroda,
Posen, Preußen
d: 26 Feb 1869
Tulce, Schroda,
Posen,Preußen

Michał Adamski
b: 12 Sep 1830
Kamin,Schimm,
Posen,Preußen
d: 06 Feb 1910
Detroit, Wayne,
Michigan, USA

Lucia Garbarek
b: 13 Dec 1835
Posen,Preußen
Rogalin, Schimm,
d: 23 Jul 1913
Detroit, Wayne,
Michigan, USA

Bartłomiej
Rychlewicz
b: Abt. 1780 Tulce,
Schroda,
Posen,Preußen
d: Aft. 1820 Tulce,
Schroda,
Posen,Preußen

Katarzyna
Nawrocka
b: 18 Mar 1792
Gowarzewo,
Schroda Posen
Preußen

Jan Szymkowiak
b: Abt. 1794 Tulce,
Schroda,
Posen,Preußen
d: 05 May 1853
Tulce, Schroda,
Posen,Preußen

Wiktoria
Sterczała
b: 28 Dec 1804
Schroda,
Posen,Preußen
d: 16 Aug 1849
Tulce, Schroda,
Posen,Preußen

Rafał Adamski
b: 30 Oct 1805
Swiontnik, Schimm,
Posen, Preußen
d: Aft. 1845
Swiatniki, Schimm,
Posen, Preußen

Zofia Smigiel
b: 08 Jan 1804
Podewow,
Posen, Schimm,
d: Swiatniki, Schimm,
Prußen, Posen,
Preußen

Wawrzyniec
Garbarek
b: Aug 1811
Rogalin, Preußen
d: 02 Dec 1876
Detroit, Preußen

Juliana
Teresińska
b: 14 Feb 1808
Rogalin, Schimm,
Posen, Preußen
d: 27 Oct 1874
Rogalin, Schimm,
Posen, Preußen

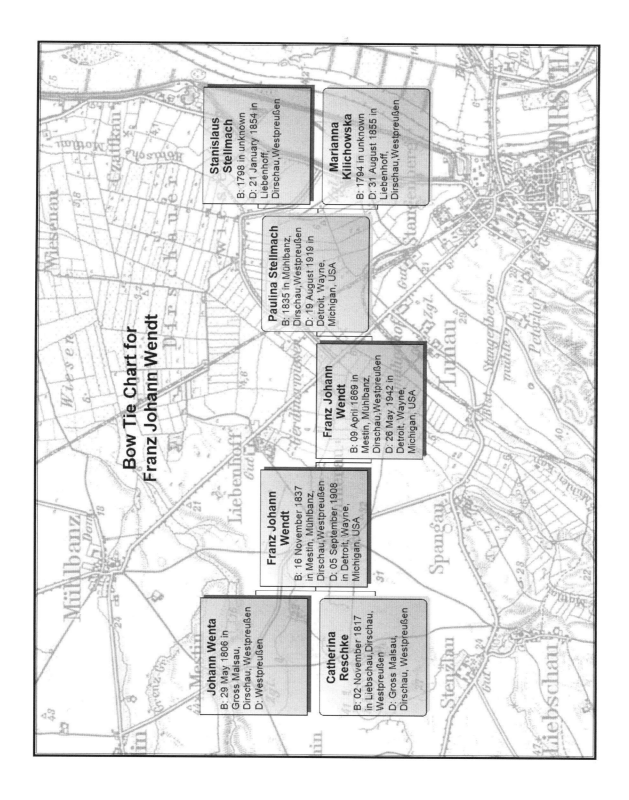

Bow Tie Chart for
Franz Johann Wendt

Stanislaus
Stellmach
B: 1798 in unknown
D: 21 January 1854 in
Liebenhoff,
Dirschau,Westpreußen

Marianna
Kilichowska
B: 1794 in unknown
D: 31 August 1855 in
Liebenhoff,
Dirschau,Westpreußen

Paulina Stellmach
B: 1835 in Mühlbanz,
Dirschau,Westpreußen
D: 19 August 1919 in
Detroit, Wayne,
Michigan, USA

Franz Johann
Wendt
B: 09 April 1869 in
Mestin, Mühlbanz,
Dirschau,Westpreußen
D: 26 May 1942 in
Detroit, Wayne,
Michigan, USA

Franz Johann
Wendt
B: 16 November 1837
in Mestin, Mühlbanz,
Dirschau,Westpreußen
D: 05 September 1908
in Detroit, Wayne,
Michigan, USA

Johann Wenta
B: 29 May 1806 in
Gross Maisau,
Dirschau, Westpreußen
D: Westpreußen

Catherina
Reschke
B: 02 November 1817
in Liebschau,Dirschau,
Westpreußen
D: Gross Maisau,
Dirschau, Westpreußen

Family Group Sheet for Anthony J. Przytulski

Husband:	Anthony J. Przytulski	
Birth:	24 Feb 1890 in Kuczbork, Żuromin, Poland	
Death:	28 Dec 1976 in Redford, Wayne, Michigan, USA	
Father:	Pater Ignotus	
Mother:	Anna Przytula	

Wife:	Cecelia Mary Wojtkowiak	
Birth:	12 Oct 1890 in Detroit, Wayne, Michigan, USA	
Death:	10 Apr 1977 in Redford, Wayne, Michigan, USA	
Father:	Piotr Wojtkowiak	
Mother:	Mariana Adamska	

Children:

1 F	Name:	Virginia Mary Przytulski
	Birth:	01 Aug 1913 in Detroit, Wayne, Michigan, USA
	Death:	23 Jun 1968 in Detroit, Wayne, Michigan, USA
	Spouse:	Albert Dominic DiNatale
2 F	Name:	Elisabeth Cecilia Przytulski
	Birth:	19 Nov 1914 in Detroit, Wayne, Michigan, USA
	Spouse:	Frank Joseph Wendt
3 F	Name:	Genevieve Teresa Przytulski
	Birth:	05 Jul 1916 in Detroit, Wayne, Michigan, USA
	Death:	23 Nov 1994 in Port Richie, Pasco, Florida, USA
	Spouse:	Bruno John Benedetti
4 M	Name:	Bernard Przytulski
	Birth:	21 May 1918 in Detroit,Wayne, Michigan, USA
	Death:	14 Dec 1921 in Detroit,Wayne, Michigan, USA
5 F	Name:	Leona Frances Przytulski
	Birth:	10 Mar 1920 in Detroit, Wayne, Michigan, USA
	Death:	28 Oct 1985 in Redford, Wayne, Michigan, USA
6 M	Name:	Anthony Joseph Przytulski
	Birth:	11 Sep 1921 in Detroit, Wayne, Michigan, USA
	Death:	09 Jan 2008 in Canton, Wayne, Michigan, USA
	Spouse:	Leocadia Victoria Stachurski
7 M	Name:	Leonard Przytulski
	Birth:	04 Sep 1923 in Detroit, Wayne, Michigan, USA
	Death:	13 Oct 1923 in Detroit, Wayne, Michigan, USA
8 F	Name:	Geraldine Theresa Przytulski
	Birth:	02 Jul 1926 in Detroit, Wayne, Michigan, USA
	Death:	22 Aug 2008 in Plymouth, Wayne, Michigan, USA
	Spouse:	Joseph Cannon
9 F	Name:	Josephine Gertrude Przytulski Kling
	Birth:	19 Mar 1928 in Detroit, Wayne, Michigan, USA
	Death:	11 Mar 2003 in Detroit, Wayne, Michigan, USA

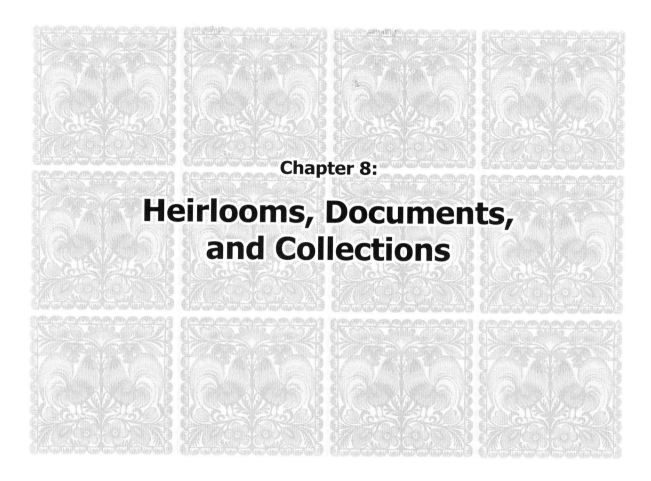

Chapter 8:

Heirlooms, Documents, and Collections

As family historians, we have an additional duty to become the family archivist. The documents, photos, and memorabilia of our ancestors must be taken out of shoe boxes and be preserved properly. It has never been easier to find the methods to make sure that future generations can enjoy your family's collection.

Family papers may include foreign passports, letters, work documents, and birth certificates created in Poland and carried by the immigrants. You will want to have them translated and store the original and English version together. Documents created in the United States may include naturalization papers, birth certificates, and marriage licenses. You may also have school books, newspaper clippings, and prayer books you wish to preserve for sentimental reasons.

These family treasures have many man-made problems. If it is not the sulfur content in the paper itself, it may be the staples, paper clips, or scotch tape that past generations have attached to the document. Sulfur leads the paper to become brittle and deteriorate. Some items may have water damage or even foxing, a discoloration of the paper due to mold.

What is the best way to store old paper items?

Is the information in the original document important? And, is it worth the cost of purchasing archival materials to store those old recipes, newspaper clippings, and journals? I think most family genealogists would not toss it at this point; but look for ways to preserve the documents. It could be microfilmed, photocopied, or sprayed with a solution available from an archival supply house which neutralizes the acid content.

There are three steps to home conservation: protection, enhancement, and inventory. Protect them by taking them out of sunlight. Take the paper out of distress by unfolding documents and storing them flat. Carefully remove staples and paper clips. Cellophane tape is a problem. Over time the tape falls away leaving behind an adhesive residue. The document is now doubly damaged—torn and contaminated with adhesive. Enhance them by cleaning and flattening the papers; and create an inventory in a software program such as Excel.

What if your documents are curled or rolled up?

Graduation diplomas fall into this category as well as large group photos. It is possible to set up a humidity chamber to treat your documents. It is up to your discretion to try the following process on your paper documents. A plastic container used to store items under beds is a good size to start with. You will need distilled water, supports to keep the paper suspended over the water, and a blotter book. You may need to gently brush the documents

with a soft brush to remove dust. The goal is to expose the paper to high humidity and allow the paper to absorb the moisture to relax the fibers. After a 48 hour treatment, the paper can be removed and gently placed into the blotter book. A clean piece of plywood or Masonite is placed onto of the blotter book and weighted down with big city sized phone books. The paper will gradually flatten and dry. Depending on the weight of the paper, it may take 48 hours to flatten. The flattened document can now be placed in an acid-free envelop and stored away from light, dust, and drying conditions. The Wisconsin Historical Society has step by step directions for creating a humidity chamber in an article

entitled *Removing Creases from Historic Papers.*
The article warns against using this technique on
unstable ink, velum, or materials that have embossed
seals on them. To store the documents after they
have been flattened, you will want to look through
archival catalogs for polyester sleeves or folders and
store the sheets in an acid-free binder or box

How do I protect Photographs and Negatives?

Photographs are a window to the past and
families can easily have photos that are 100 years
old. Families have carte de viste photos that were
taken by a professional photographer and mounted
on paper board. They were a popular form used by
portrait studios during the 1860-1880s. They are
basically 2.1″ x 3.5″ mounted on a card 2.5″ x 4″. Cabinet cards followed carte de viste and
are 4.5″ x 6.5″. Some were mounted on plain boards. As the form developed the cards not
only identified the photographer and studio; but had ornate advertising on the back. This
information is very useful in pinpointing the area the family lived at the time the photo was
taken. Check out the *Dead Fred Genealogy Photo Archive* site. ***www.deadfred.com***

Box Cameras

When families bought their own Kodak box camera, their collection expanded to more
informal photos. You may have a range of print and negative sizes. Many of these turn of
the century family photos are in a vertical format which was the standard way to hold the
box camera. Negatives should be removed from the commercial paper and plastic sleeves.
Index and store them in acid and lignin-free safe sleeves. If archival materials are not readily
available in your community, you can order them online at Light Impressions or Lumiere
Photo. ***www.lightimpressionsdirect.com*** and ***www.lumierephoto.com***

Scanners

Many family genealogists purchase a scanner that has an adapter which allows for the
scanning of 120 and 35 mm format negatives. Coupled with a software program like *Adobe
Photoshop Elements,* a scanner can help create a home studio capable of enlarging, repairing,
and sharing family photos. ***www.adobe.com/products/tips/photoshopelwin.html***

Identification and Storage

Photos, like documents, should be kept out of light and protected in acid-free sleeves and binders or boxes. The photos need to be identified. The National Archives advises using a soft pencil to write on the back of the photo. Do not put a sticker on the back because over time the adhesives will dry and the label will fall off. Most photos printed since the 1960s are printed on resin-coated paper and acid-free pens are available that write on this surface. Care must be taken to write in the margin of the photo and not in the middle. It is easy to press too hard and emboss the surface of the photo. Let the ink dry before handling the photo to avoid smudging. Photos can be placed back to back before being placed in a polyester sleeve. It is best to display a reproduction of the photo and put the original in safekeeping. Avoid storing your photo collection in the basement or attic. The driest and most evenly tempered room is the area you will want.

www.archives.gov/preservation/family-archives

How do I care for Fabrics?

The family archive may also have military uniforms, wedding dresses, baptismal gowns, and women's crafts such as crocheting, knitting, and embroidery. Be sure to document the history of each item and include family stories that explain their importance. Nonagerian, Elizabeth Przytulska Wendt, recalls that her mother had sewn the christening gown for her

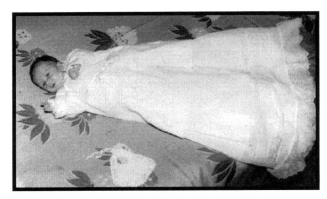

Anthony and Cecelia Przytulski's grandson, Alan (1946), was also baptized in this gown.

first born in 1913. Each payday Cecilia Wojtkowiak Przytulska used an allotted sum to purchase lace or material for the gown. The restored cotton batiste christening gown is about 2.5 feet in length and there are two slips. The first slip was made of cotton since first born, Virginia, was baptized in August; and the winter slip of wool was made for the second child, Elizabeth, who was born in November, 1914. Cecilia had used her wedding veil as netting on the baby carriage. Boys and girls alike wore the Christening gown. All 9 of Tony and Cecilia's children were baptized in the gown, starting a family tradition. Use of the gown continued into the next generation for their 26 grandchildren. Many great-grandchildren were also baptized in it.

Rebirth

The gown was retired and almost forgotten due to the fragility of the fabric and changing fashion. The baptismal outfit was found in the back of a closet in a dusty cardboard box. It was labeled *"Christening Dress, Made by Cecilia Przytulski, June-July, 1913."* The tissue paper had yellowed and pieces of polyester lace had been used to patch the wear and tear. Small hangers were in the box along with a list of all the babies who were christened in the gown. Because of the rich tradition of the gown, a professional conservator was hired to revive and conserve the three piece outfit. The batiste garments were laundered in a gentle solution. The wool slip was simply vacuumed with a minimum suction, using a screen over the fabric for protection. The conservator removed the polyester lace and mended the tears in the delicate fabric. An identifying label of unbleached muslin bearing Cecilia's name and the date it was sown was attached to the outfit in an inconspicuous spot. When the process was completed, the set was placed in a museum storage box with acid-free tissue between each piece. It was an expensive process; but to borrow an expression from a current commercial, *"To have a garment with such a rich family history: Priceless!"* The preservation was so successful that the gown was used most recently in 2009 for the baptism of Virginia's great-grandson.

I put the story and photos of the gown on my Web site and an interested viewer, NanaPennyPockets, wrote: *"Thank you so much for that site! I have a night gown worn by my great-aunt for her wedding with many of the laces shown in the dress and it helped me date the nightgown! Thank you for sharing that with us! Also a great reminder to label our gowns with not only the name, but the year we made them so hopefully future generations can share in passing them down!"*

How do I safeguard my Digital Data?

While you are using state of the art technology today for record keeping and backup storage, you need to remember how technology formats fade away. Are you going to continually move files to newer formats; or, like archives and museums, maintain "antique" equipment to access data in earlier formats? A student in 2002 was perplexed when instructed to use a typewriter. She said, *"Wow! It's a computer without the monitor."* In any case, you need to consider auxiliary hard drives, storage of files on gold DVDs, or perhaps the exploration of an online backup service such as Mozy. ***www.mozy.com***

How do I select an appropriate museum or archive to donate my collection?

Here is a case study for you to consider. J. William Gorski shared his decision making process with me and explained why he selected two locations, the Library of Michigan and the Archives of Michigan, as the repository for his personal collection. The majority of the holdings documented Polish history and genealogy in the state of Michigan, with special emphasis on the metropolitan Detroit area. Resources include Polish newspapers, church jubilee books, local histories, and slides and photographs. Bill Gorski became interested in his Polish heritage in 1977. He was a skilled tradesman at Fisher Body in Detroit and the editor of the Polish Genealogical Society of Michigan's journal, *The Polish Eaglet*. During the 1970s he worked closely with fellow genealogist, Pam Lazar, traveling around the state photographing portraits on Polish-American tombstones. Many of the stones have since been defaced. Bill's collection also includes over 250 parish jubilee books from Michigan and Ontario. His passion for photography resulted in 3,500 slides which include stained glass windows and church interiors, a number of which have been razed.

Bill contacted a range of parochial and public archives and universities. Some were lukewarm to the collection and one curator never arrived to a pre-arranged meeting. So, when he had a positive and cooperative response from the Library and Archives of Michigan, he knew he had found a home for the collection. He envisioned all the materials being shelved together; but that was not possible. Most archives and libraries reserve the right to use the donated collection in the way it will maximize research for patrons. He funded and prepared hard bound copies of the catalog. Gorski was able to claim a tax deduction on the collection that was valued at $30,000 in 2002.

Are there donation guidelines?

Many libraries and archives have developed guidelines for donations. Provided below are some pointers from the Library of Congress in Washington, D.C. and the Family History Library in Salt Lake City, Utah.

Library of Congress

You can donate your family's genealogy or local history to the Library of Congress by mail. Donations to the Library of Congress will be acknowledged, and may be tax deductible, depending on the donor's own tax situation. The library strongly encourages the use of acid-free paper; and if the work requires binding, allow wide margins.

Library of Congress
Local History and Genealogy, Collection Development
101 Independence Avenue SE
Washington, DC 20540-4660

Visit their online site for more information. *www.loc.gov/rr/genealogy/gifts/html*

The Family History Library

All donations become the property of the FHL. The material must be legible and help researchers identify individuals by name, date, and place. The following is a modified extraction from *Guidelines: Donations to the Family History Library*. The library accepts: family histories with genealogical information, genealogical periodicals, cemetery records, church records, church histories, court records, and vital records. On a limited basis and with prior approval the library accepts: local histories, indexes to records, passenger lists, naturalization records, military records, newspaper extracts, and land records. Autobiographies with genealogical material will also be accepted. If possible, send an unbound, double sided copy of your manuscript. Unbound manuscripts are easier to microfilm and double sided manuscripts take less shelf space. The library accepts family histories on disc; but paper is preferred. The library does accept photocopies of genealogical information written in a family bible by a family. If possible send a photocopy of the bible's title page and the owner's name and address. Materials the library does not accept include: personal journals, school yearbooks, correspondence, and travelogues. They do not collect artifacts, memorabilia, photo albums, scrapbooks, or works of fiction. In addition, materials may be loaned to the library for microfilming. After permission is given, the library does the filming and returns the originals. Patrons send the materials at their own expense.

www.familysearch.org/eng/Search/RG/images/FamilySearch_Donation_Guidelines_rev_5-09.pdf

The library pays for the microfilming and the return of the material. The owner may request a courtesy copy of the microfilm. For further information contact:

Family History Library
Gifts or Patron Microfilming [select the correct item]
35 North West Temple Street
Salt Lake City, UT 84150-3400
email: hfl@ldschurch.org

Are there any Polish-American repositories interested in Genealogy?

The Polish Mission associates its history with the founding of SS Cyril and Methodius Seminary which was opened in Detroit in 1885. The institution moved to Orchard Lake, Michigan in 1909 and shares the grounds with St. Mary's Preparatory High School and the Central Archives of Polonia. The Polish Mission organizes programs and events that highlight Polish and Pol-Am culture and accomplishments. The private archives of Orchard Lake Schools has opened its holdings to the public via the 501(c)(3) Polish Mission and the Polonica Americana Research Institute (PARI). The Research Institute is a subsidiary of the Polish Mission and functions under the direction of Cecile (Ceil) Wendt Jensen, Certified Genealogist[SM]. PARI offers lectures, seminars, society visits, and individual research packages. Volunteers at PARI employ professional techniques of record transcription and extraction from original Polish and Pol-Am records to benefit Polonia. They specialize in identifying ancestral villages.

What type of records does PARI hold?

A short list of PARI record sets ready for indexing and digitizing includes: Michigan sponsors of World War II Displaced Persons; late 19th century enrollment cards and composite photos for SS Cyril and Methodius Seminary students; late 19th century enrollment cards and candid photos for students at St. Mary's Preparatory High School; 1922 letters written by Polish school children thanking the United States for support during World War I (a similar collection is held by the Library of Congress in Washington, D.C.). October is Polish Heritage Month and events are held to showcase how Polish descendants impacted Michigan's farming, mining, forestry, industry, and politics.

What type of records does PARI collect?

PARI is currently accepting materials relevant to genealogy. The scope covers a diverse range of materials produced by North American Polonia together with key institutions—churches, schools, organizations, and the press. Specific items of interest from these institutions include: jubilee books; parish histories; prayer books; parish bulletins; materials

Two of the priests identified in the photo above include:
Bishop Michael J. Gallagher, Bishop of Detroit and Bishop Joseph C. Plagens.

pertaining to the Roman Catholic and Polish National Catholic Church; Polonian school yearbooks, anniversary brochures, school programs, and student albums; publications of Religious Orders; newspapers; magazines; flyers and books in both English and Polish; biographical materials; correspondence; memorabilia; obituaries; and funeral cards. Addtionally, PARI is interested in: vintage photos as well as digital scans of photos and negatives; maps; postcards; passports; and civil and religious certificates. Families are encouraged to submit family histories and family group sheets. At this time, PARI is not purchasing materials, and asks that a donation accompany the collection to purchase the appropriate archival materials for proper preservation. Staff members can be consulted with regards to related costs. Please call 248.683.0412 or visit *www.polishmission.com*

Email: Marcin Chumiecki, Polish Mission Director, at mchumiecki@orchardlakeschools. com or Ceil Wendt Jensen, PARI Director, at cjensen@mipolonia.net.

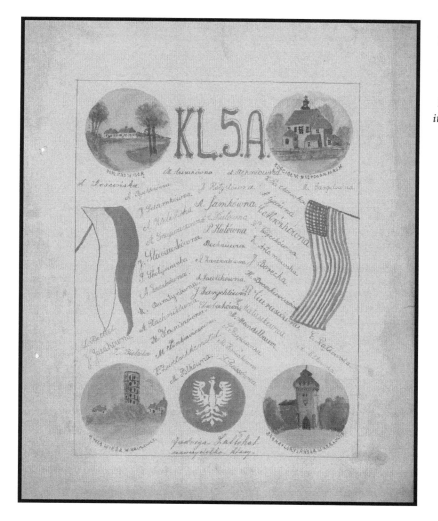

This greeting from Class 5 in Niepołomice was sent to the U.S. in 1922, expressing their thanks to Polonia for relief support after World War I.
Illustrated by the school children, it is one of 210 pages in a collection held at the Polish Mission.

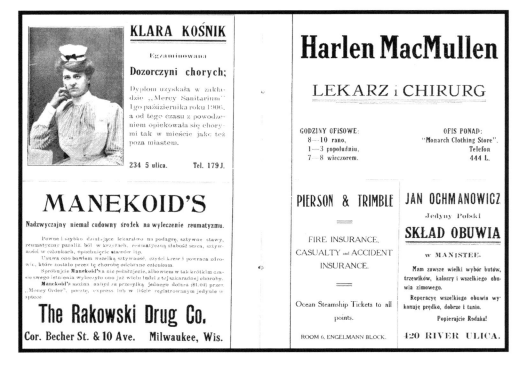

*Jubilee books are usually published by parishes on anniversaries and funded
by community advertisements. You may find your family listed in the business
ads of the booklet. Pictured here are ads featured in the Manistee and Milwaukee
Jubilee books held in the Polish Mission collection.*

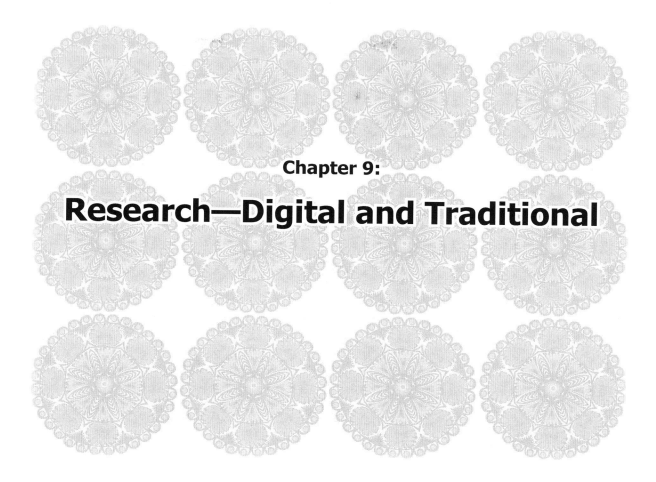

Chapter 9:
Research—Digital and Traditional

I think everyone likes something for free. So, we are going to start this chapter on digital and traditional research by introducing some new Web sites and tools while reviewing a few sites written about in earlier chapters. There are three products offered by Google that, when used in unison, will give the family historian a Web presence for free. By using keywords, Geo tags, and labels, the content you are developing is rapidly added to Google's indexes. This includes not only text; but images, videos, and audio files you may have embedded in your Web site or blog.

Let us independently look at the three tools that I like to call the Google triangle and then see how they work seamlessly to give you a custom state of the art Web presence. We will start with Gmail. Even if you have another email account, you may want to dedicate one specifically for genealogy. Gmail allows you to create a free account, although you do need to enter an additional email address as a contact. Before you open the account, think ahead. If this is going to be an account for your genealogical research, you may want to use one of your ancestral surnames or regions as part of the email address.

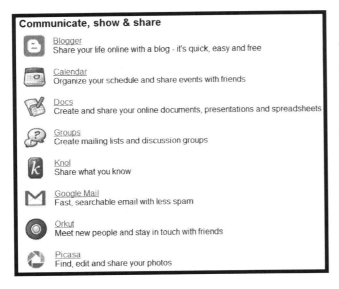

Communicate, show & share

Blogger
Share your life online with a blog - it's quick, easy and free

Calendar
Organize your schedule and share events with friends

Docs
Create and share your online documents, presentations and spreadsheets

Groups
Create mailing lists and discussion groups

Knol
Share what you know

Google Mail
Fast, searchable email with less spam

Orkut
Meet new people and stay in touch with friends

Picasa
Find, edit and share your photos

If you want to be taken seriously, avoid using email addresses such as roadrage1957@gmail.com. The Gmail account has many nice features including a spam filter to keep out unwanted email, a spell check, and if you are writing to another Gmail user, you know that the Polish diacritical you enter in your email will be legible in theirs. The Gmail account is your gateway to additional tools such as a calendar, photo albums that can be private or public, and an area to store or share documents, presentations, and spreadsheets. An interesting feature of the documents area is that you can share the document with another researcher; and you can both edit the same document in real time. Because it is color-coded, you will know which partner edited the new information. Google also offers a social networking tool called Buzz that combines the separate elements of Gmail and allows you to communicate, show, and share your content. ***www.gmail.google.com***

Now it is time to download some Google software—Picasa, a photo editor and organizer. While not as robust as other photo and graphic editing software, it does offer most of the components you need. You can clean up redeye, crop and straighten a photo, and adjust contrast and balance. It also allows you to add a soft focus to your image; or apply a sepia tone to vintage photos and maps. Picasa includes features that allow you to create a collage of photos, animate them for upload to the Web site, *YouTube*, and share pictures with captions in a Web album. Picasa also allows you to bring images in from your scanner, smart phone, or digital camera. Where was this software when I was still teaching in the public school classroom? ***www.picasa.google.com***

The third part of the Google triangle is their Blogger utility. Google describes a blog as an easy to make Web site, where you can quickly post thoughts and interact with people —all for free. You need to have a Gmail account to set up your Blogger. Once again, you need to think ahead and decide on the subject of your blog—is it going to be for your genealogy society, your personal research, or perhaps your ancestral region? The blog allows you to publish your ideas, control the type of feedback you receive, post photos, and share documents and other ephemera. It can be password protected to collaborate with a limited audience or set to public view for an expansive community. As soon as your account is set up, you will be able to select the template for your blog. While Blogger offers some flashy selections, it is more prudent to create a welcoming site that has a light background with dark

fonts for contrast. *www.blogger.com*

The Polish Pioneers of Calumet, Michigan is a blog devoted to a community of miners. It was created by using Google's Gmail, Picasa, and Blogger. Let us look at some individual components. The Gmail account was set up with the regional description—calumetmi@gmail.com. Then, the template was selected with the graphics being edited in Picasa. Finally, the illustration and images were uploaded to the photo album. You can see on the home page that there is an embedded slide show. It can be set to automatically advance, and when clicked on, expand to a full screen complete with forward, pause, and review buttons. There is also a static image of the Baranowski portraits. Labels that you create under each of the posts help the Google search engine index your material. The Pioneer Poles blog

displays links to collections of documents organized in Gmail. If you click on the homestead records for Joe Adamski, the Picasa photo album will open allowing you to enlarge and read the paperwork he filed when he purchased land in the Upper Peninsula of Michigan. *www.calumetmi.blogspot.com*

There are several other Google offerings that will help enhance your blog such as Google's Maps, Earth, and Toolbar. Google Earth can be overlaid with David Rumsey's vintage maps of Poland showing the old borders with the current country boundaries. The directions on how to use Google Earth and the collection can be found online. *www.earth.google.com* and *http://rumsey.geogarage.com/gmaps.html*

The United Polish Genealogical Societies used Google Maps to pinpoint the Polish villages the attendees were researching. As with most Internet tools, you can share as little or as much data as you like. *www.maps.google.com* and *www.upgs.wordpress.com/2008/02/12/wheres-your-ancestral-village*

While I think Google tools are easy to use, priced right, and a great way to share your research, there are other online services such as WordPress. Your own Internet service

provider, such as Comcast, may offer free Web space for you to develop a site or blog.

In 2010 Family Tree Magazine recognized three Polish-American genealogists who have developed blogs that are worth reading and emulating. Steve Danko brings his scientific background to his genealogical research; and his posts on *Steve's Genealogy Blog* chronicle the challenges of research in Lithuania and Poland. He was in the Heritage category. *www.stephendanko.com*

Donna Pointkouski's blog won in the Personal and Family category and is entitled *What's Past is Prologue* (a little nod to the engraving on the building of the National Archives in Washington, D.C.). Her posts include interviews with leading Polish-American researchers, documents from her Polish and German heritage, and short stories based on her childhood. Donna's blog is hosted by WordPress. *www.pastprologue.wordpress.com*

I am pleased to mention Jasia, who is a recipient of the All-Around category of the 40 Best Genealogy Blogs awards. I meet with her periodically to compare our West Side Detroit history. *The Creative Gene* showcases her digital photography and scrap booking talents. Her site is always current, and she writes about family matters with insight, creativity, and humor. Jasia has also created Web sites for three Polish parishes in Detroit: St. Albertus, St. Josephat, and Sweetest Heart of Mary. *www.creativegene.blogspot.com*

How can I find people who would like to collaborate on research?

Another gold standard is RootsWeb. It is the Internet's oldest and largest free genealogical community offering searchable databases, active and archived emailing lists, and even free Web space for genealogical societies and projects. The home page offers several online guides including Getting Started at RootsWeb and RootsWeb Guide to Tracing Family Trees. The top toolbar offers the choices **Searches**, **Trees**, **Mailing Lists**, **Message Boards**, and **Web Sites**. This is one of the first Web sites I access when beginning research for a new client or patron. The search engines allow me to access surname lists, the Social Security Death Index, and U.S. town and county databases. RootsWeb's WorldConnect Project allows me to search family trees that individual researchers have uploaded to the site. The mailing lists are a great place to get the pulse of the Polish genealogical community. You can join a general topic mailing list such as Polish-Roots or a very specific email list such as Pol-Rzeszow. You

will receive a copy of each email that is posted to the list. There are two options to receiving the email. The "list" option sends you each email when posted. If you are worried about being overwhelmed by too many messages, select the "digest mode" and the emails will be bundled which makes it easier to follow the conversations. You need to learn the manners or netiquette of a list, which will define for you off-topic subjects, rules about advertising, and flaming. It is also a good idea to search or browse the archived messages. I have noticed over time that more researchers in Poland are participating in these mailing lists. You will find knowledgeable researchers who are willing to take a look at your document, advise you on finding a Polish tour guide or researcher, or perhaps offer ideas to bring down the genealogical brick walls you may encounter.

When working with patrons, I suggest they search the message boards and see if anyone else is searching for the same family line. If there is not a message board for their surname, I encourage them to request RootsWeb to set one up. You need a free RootsWeb account to set up a new board. Since RootsWeb is owned by Ancestry, you can use that login if you are a subscriber. Requests for the creation of a new board may be submitted for the following topics:

Surname - Requests must be for a single surname only.

Localities - Suggested localities are countries, states, provinces, departments, shires, counties/parishes, or similar.

Genealogical Research Topics - Requested topics must be specific subjects that would be of interest to a number of researchers.

You have the opportunity to become the administrator of the board and prime the pump by posting a few messages that include queries, known facts, or useful resources. I personally had

The Thomas Zdziebko family from Zarzecze, Jasło, Galicia.
The family came to the United Sates in 1880.
This circa 1912 portrait of the family was obtained from
a long lost cousin who was located via the Zdziebko
surname board on Rootsweb.

great results by setting up a surname message board. While my first few posts took a year to garner replies, I was pleased to be able to link up with several first cousins including one who lived six doors away. *http://boards. rootsweb.com/requestboard.aspx*

Are there other online resources for genealogy?

Another useful Web site is *Random Acts of Genealogical Kindness.* Researchers around the country and in some cases, around the globe, are willing to do a bit of research for you. You can request a snapshot of a tombstone from a cemetery in their area or perhaps a look up at a local library; but not information on living people or those looking for their birth parents. Of course there are a few guidelines that remind you to limit your query to one request. Be sure to render a small fee if required and offer a thank you when a task is accomplished. *www.raogk.org*

If you cannot make it to a regional seminar, then they can come to you. Known as Webinars, these online lectures often feature graphics as well as audio and can be downloaded to your computer or smart phone. Some well known Podcasters include *Dear Myrtle*, site name and nom de plume of Pat Richley-Erickson; and George G. Morgan and Drew Smith, who produce *The Genealogy Guys Podcast. www.dearmyrtle.com* and *www.genealogyguys.com*

What do I do when I come to a "dead end" in my research?

One of the best things about researching family history in the 21st century is that we can have a foot in both the traditional discipline and digital methodology. One of my favorite places to research is in the local history room at the public library. This is where you get to meet the know-it-alls, and I mean this in the best possible way. These people know where the regional resources and records are kept. While researching in a mining community in northern Michigan, I met a man who knew the holdings of the local historical societies like the back of his hand. In minutes, he showed me where to find the obituaries I was seeking.

He even identified the storefront pictured in my 1920s photograph. He mentioned that his earlier career as a mailman gave him a mental directory of all the buildings on Main Street. A similar situation happened in Poland. I casually mentioned my interest in school records to a local family historian while waiting for our entrée in a restaurant. Before

Header of Der Michigan Wegweiser (Michigan Guidebook).
The illustration pictorially conveys the wealth that awaits the immigrant if they settle in the state. On the left, the year 1870 is portrayed with a log cabin near a stream. The year 1880 is depicted on the other side of the Great Seal of the State of Michigan by a fine two story home. From the Archives of Michigan Executive Office record group.

dessert was served, Krzysztof made a round trip to a friend's home, and returned with a teacher's ledger under his arm. On page 26 was an entry for my uncle listing his grade level, age, and classmates.

This section cannot end without mentioning a traditional and very useful service from your public library. Try using their Interlibrary loan service. You start by searching a broad range of libraries with *WorldCat*. Your search results can be sorted by location showing the libraries closest to you that hold the materials of interest. There is usually a small fee required to have the resources sent to your library where you can use them for a limited period of time. In most cases the materials cannot be taken home. I requested a microfilm of the publication circulated by a U. S. immigration agent seeking to bring Prussian citizens to the Midwest in the 1870s. Coupled with primary documents found at the state archives, I could recreate the sales pitch given to my ancestors to encourage them to come to America. ***www.worldcat.org***

Just as with public libraries, the Family History Library and its branches offer patrons free access to some subscription databases. Currently, your local FHC not only provides their FamilySearch catalog and Research Guidance; but also AncestryInstitution, Footnote, and WorldVitalRecords. Volunteers can help you get acclimated to using the facilities and databases, offer suggestions of sources for you to search, and answer basic genealogical questions. They will not do the research for you.

Are there any software programs for genealogy?

Ancestry provides family researchers with powerful software and Web sites to streamline the research, sharing, and publication of family histories. I have been using Family Tree Maker (FTM) software for more than ten years. Over time, I have seen the program change from a database for pedigree storage to its current ability to interface with *Ancestry.com*. Some researchers feel overwhelmed when using new technology. I did too, when I first started using computers in 1980. I was motivated to go digital the day I was denied No. 2 pencils for my drawing class. The secretary said I was over my budget (it was January!) and as fate would have it there was a district announcement in my mailbox about the forthcoming multi-million dollar technology plan. Seeking teaching materials, I went to the first workshop. I had my hands full booting up my Amiga 500 with a workbench disk and left the 1200 baud modem in the closet for a year. The "handshake" of initializing the modem over a phone line sounded like something from outer space.

Over time, I learned to scan photos, upload files, and launch my own Web site complete with digital videos. You can do it too. It just takes time and perhaps a session or two with a child or grandchild. You will not be the only one getting family support. In his book *Click*, author Bill Tancer tracked spikes in uploads to an online video site by 45-54 year olds during the summer as well as winter and spring break (times when their Gen X children were home). Whether you are an early, middle, or late adapter of software and technology, the research results achieved using the Ancestry products will hook you faster than you can say "Who's your Daddy?"

Is Martha Stewart my Cousin?

FTM is my mainstay software when I begin research for a new client. Recently, I read that Martha Stewart was visiting Poland, the birthplace of her grandparents. I wondered what I could find out about her lineage—perhaps we shared an ancestral village or two. I became more conscious of my research techniques as I began the Stewart project. I realize I moved between the search function in the FTM software and the actual Ancestry site. FTM will search the following online sites: *Ancestry.com*, *Rootsweb.com*, and *Genealogy.com*, as well as other search engines: *Google.com*, *Yahoo.com*, and *LiveSearch.com*. The only online Stewart pedigree I could find was on *Genealogy.com* and it was lacking citations and had noticeable misspellings.

I found the 2007 obituary of Stewart's mother, Martha R. Kostyra, via Ancestry and used it as a starting point. The obituary for Big Martha, as she was affectionately known, ran in many newspapers across the country and was edited in each paper's style. I gained a little more information with each obit. It is always "a good thing" to read as many versions of an obituary as possible. Kostyra's husband, Edward, died in 1979 and I found her maiden name: Ruszkowski (her brother was listed with a shortened form, Russ). She was Catholic, had six children, and lived in New York, New Jersey, and Connecticut during her lifetime. That was important information which enabled me to find these U.S. families' census records. I searched using Big Martha's maiden name for the family's 1930 U.S. census. I repeated the search for her husband, Edward Kostyra. The search results gave me good information and I began to fill in the pedigree chart, on the **Getting Started** page of FTM .

With three names and dates entered on the pedigree chart a green leaf displayed indicating possible matches in the Ancestry database. I found Edward Kostyra's entry in the Social Society Death Index and used the merge feature in the software to bring the data into the program. The following source-citation was automatically generated:

- Ancestry.com, Social Security Death Index (Provo, UT, USA: The Generations Network, Inc., 2008), Database online. Record for Edward Kostyra.

FTM's **Merge Wizard** allows editing this citation to the format used by professional genealogists:

- U.S. Social Security Administration, "Social Security Death Index", database, Ancestry.com (*http://ancestry.com*: accessed 15 December 2008), entry for Edward Kostyra, no. 110-18-7944.

Since my goal was to compare ancestral villages, I needed to find Martha's immigrant ancestors' names and ship manifests. By refreshing the search within FTM, additional documents, including the World War II Draft registration of Frank Kostyra listing Kopki, Poland as his birthplace, were found. The 1930 census identified Frank Kostyra as head of the family, 50 years of age, and listed his place of birth as Austrian-Kopke, with the immigration date of 1905. It is unusual to find the name of the village entered, misspelled as it was.

I hit a snag looking for the Kostyra and Ruszkowski manifests. I had to change their Anglicized given names to the Polish form in the search engine. When I changed the place of birth to the place of residence, I also gained more records. To avoid changing an entry in FTM and forgetting to change it back to the preferred entry, I switched to using *Ancestry.com* directly to find additional documents.

I found Big Martha's census information by using her last name, birth year, and the location of Buffalo, New York. She was listed in the 1930 census as Harriet Ruszkowski. I left the Ancestry site to check the Erie County Clerk database for naturalization papers. I found that some of the given name confusion might have stemmed from her Polish baptismal name of Jadwiga, listed on her father's naturalization papers. I found this information with the help of Linda Drake, Senior Documents Clerk, at the Erie County Clerk's Office and their online database. *http://ecclerk.erie.gov*

```
            ERIE COUNTY CLERK'S OFFICE
            OFFICIAL RECORDS PUBLIC SEARCH
Search Results                              Logout

DOCUMENT DETAIL: (M)
Doc Type:       990
Doc Group:      CITZ
CFN:            200102060689
Date/Time:      06/08/1925  :
Book Type:
Book/Page:      /
Pages:          0
Original Amt:   $0.00
Original Date:
Stated Amt:     $0.00
Misc:           16295
Status:         B
Index Seq:
Case #:         000000

                Parties
D  RUSZKOWSKI JOSEPH
R  RUSZKOWSKI FRANCES
R  RUSZKOWSKI JADWIGA
R  RUSZKOWSKI EUGENE
R  RUSZKOWSKI ALEXANDER
R  RUSZKOWSKI CLEMENTINE

Long Legal 1 Town Map/Hostel/Parcel Zip Prop Type
                                         1
```

The naturalization record had additional geographic information that helped sort out the Ruszkowski ancestral village of Kotuń. The search within FTM brought up a 6 September 1910 ship manifest for Josef Ruszkowski, birth about 1889, nativity Russia, which fit his description. However, when I read the actual manifest, this Ruszkowski was heading to Chicago. I needed someone bound for Buffalo. I continued the search by hitting the button **Show More**, and the correct manifest was linked. It was his record: Josef Ruszkowski, birth about 1889, with his New York arrival on 18 September 1910 sailing from Hamburg on the *SS Cincinnati*. He was bound for the home of his cousin, Jan Ruszkowski, in Buffalo, New York. I was successful in finding the ship manifests for all of Martha Stewart's grandparents and stored the documents found online in the **Media** folder of FTM.

The software's **Places** function allowed me to correctly identify and then plot the ancestral villages using the **Map** feature in FTM. I used Microsoft's online tool, **Live Search Maps**, to create a composite map (featured on page 125) in order to compare village locations and add multiple push pins and boundary lines. Microsoft also offers the **Map Crunching** feature, which allows a vintage map to be superimposed over the current boundaries.

Legend: **Stewart villages** 1. Kopki (Kostyra); 2. Zagórze (Krukar); 3. Kotuń (Ruszkowski); 4. Janów (Albiniak); **Jensen villages** 5. Rogalinek (Adamski); 6. Zarzecze (Zdziebko); 7. not shown Miłobądz (Wendt); 8. Kuczbork (Przytulski); 9. Villages 1,2,3, and 4 are the ancestral villages of Martha Kostyra Stewart

Once the map with pushpins marking ancestral villages was completed, I used the **Draw a Path** tool to calculate the distance between our closest villages: 64 miles. I used the **Share** command in FTM to post the Stewart pedigree on Ancestry along with all the documents from the **Media** folder. You can find it online as Kostyra with the note: This tree was created using U.S. documents. The Polish parish records should be checked to verify the Kostyra, Ruszkowski, Krukar, and Albiniak family locations in Poland.

Genealogical Codicil

According to the Merriam-Webster Dictionary, a codicil is a legal instrument made to modify an earlier will. Anyone who is doing genealogical research needs to prepare a codicil to their will if their research has not already been included in their Last Will and Testament. Having spent a lot of time, effort, and money on your research, you certainly would not want it to get lost or destroyed. The wording can be adjusted to fit your particular situation. A lawyer can certainly help you with the specific wording and have it filed with your will. Here is a modified example that may be found online.
www. rootsweb.ancestry.com/~alwalker/Codicil.htm

To my spouse, children, guardian, administrator, and executor:
Upon my demise, it is requested that you do not dispose of any of my genealogical records, either those prepared personally by me or those records prepared by others, which may be in my possession including, but not limited to—books, files, notebooks, or computer programs—for a period of two years. During this time period, please attempt to identify one or more persons who would be willing to take custody of the said materials and the responsibility of maintaining and continuing the family histories. [If you know whom within your family or friends are likely candidates to accept these materials, please add the following at this point: "I suggest that the persons contacted regarding the assumption of the custody of these items include but not be limited to" and then list the names of those individuals at this point, with their addresses and telephone numbers, if known].

In the event you do not find anyone to accept these materials, please contact the various genealogical organizations that I have been a member of and determine if they will accept some parts or all of my genealogical materials [List the local organizations or chapters, as well as state and national groups you would prefer to have contacted regarding your genealogical records. Include current addresses, phone numbers, and contact persons].

Please remember that my genealogical endeavors consumed a great deal of time, travel, and money. Therefore, it is my desire that the products of these endeavors be allowed to continue in a manner that will make them available to others in the future.

Signature _____ Date _____

Witness _____ Date _____

Witness _____ Date _____

Web Addresses

Chapter 1: Polish Communities and Societies

www.pgsa.org

www.pgsca.org

www.freewebs.com/pgsgc

www.pgsctne.org

www.rootsweb.com/~mapgsm

www.pgsm.org

www.rootsweb.com/~mnpolgs/pgs-mn.html

www.pgsnys.org

www.pgst.org

www.tpgs02.org

www.iajgs.org

www.sggee.org

www.mennonitechurch.ca/programs/archives

www.lemko.org

Chapter 2: Foundation Research

www.footnote.com

www.ancestry.com

www.stevemorse.org

www.familyhistory.hhs.gov

www.hhs.gov/familyhistory/downloads/portraitEng.pdf

www.vitalchek.com

www.wisconsinhistory.org

www.familysearch.org

www.usgenweb.org

www.pgsa.org

www.interment.net

www.findagrave.com

www.gravestonestudies.org

www.pgsa.org/PDFs/DzChicObit.pdf

Chapter 3: U.S. Military Records

www.pgsa.org/haller.php

www.ancestry.com

www.bentley.umich.edu

www.abmc.gov/home.php

www.cem.va.gov

www.polishroots.com/Resources/swap_lodges/tabid/273/Default.aspx

www.pava-swap.org/muzeum/folder.htm

Chapter 4: Immigration and Naturalization

www.ancestry.com

www.footnote.com

www.worldvitalrecords.com

www.uscis.gov/genealogy

http://ecclerk.erie.gov:9080/prod_public_view/login.jsp

www.germanroots.com/passengers.html

www.galvestonhistory.org/Galveston_Immigration_Database.asp

www.theshipslist.com

www.stevemorse.org

www.anthonj.de/genealogen

www.passagierlisten.de

www.jewishgen.org/infofiles/Manifests/occ

Chapter 5: Geography, Gazetteers, and Maps

www.mapa.szukacz.pl

www.pgsa.org/Maps/polishatlas.php

www.feefhs.org/maplibrary/russian/re-polan.html

www.library.wisc.edu/etext/ravenstein/home.html

www.adobe.com

http://lazarus.elte.hu/hun/gb/maps.htm

www.moikrewni.pl/mapa

www.herby.com.pl

www.jewishgen.org/Communities

www.polishroots.org

www.Kartenmeister.com

www.mapywig.org

www.loc.gov./rr/askalib

legacy.www.nypl.org/research/chss/jws/yizkorbookonline.cfm

www.hantman.net/geneology/LittmanStory/story.htm

Chapter 6: Record Keeping and Handwriting in Poland

www.jewishgen.org/infofiles/polandv.html

www.zbc.uz.zgora.pl

www.familysearch.org

www.sggee.org/research/translation_aids

www.script.byu.edu/german/en/welcome.aspx

www.archiwa.gov.pl/lang-en/for-archive-users/genealogy/407-types-of-sources-used-for-genealogical-queries.html

Chapter 7: Case Studies and Historical Documents

www.archiwa.gov.pl

www.stolat-jensen.blogspot.com

www.wyspaedwarda.jms.pl/wypoczni.htm

www.krzysztofkowalkowski.pl

www.cepr.pl

www.tachna.com

www.zchor.org/tachna.htm

www.polishroots.com/Resources/austrian_recruit/tabid/204/Default.aspx

www.iabsi.com/gen/public/ahm.html

www.kresy-siberia.org

www.polishmission.com

www.archives.gov/research/ww2/refugees.html

www.its-arolsen.org

www.avotaynu.com/magnates.htm

Chapter 8: Heirlooms, Documents, and Collections

www.deadfred.com

www.lightimpressionsdirect.com

www.lumierephoto.com

www.adobe.com/products/tips/photoshopelwin.html

www.archives.gov/preservation/family-archives

www.mozy.com

www.loc.gov/rr/genealogy/gifts/html
www.familysearch.org/eng/Search/RG/images/FamilySearch_Donation_Guidelines_rev_5-09.pdf
www.polishmission.com

Chapter 9: Research—Digital and Traditonal
www.gmail.google.com
www.picasa.google.com
www.blogger.com
www.calumetmi.blogspot.com
www.earth.google.com
http://rumsey.geogarage.com/gmaps.html
www.stephendanko.com
www.pastprologue.wordpress.com
www.creativegene.blogspot.com
www.raogk.org
www.dearmyrtle.com
www.genealogyguys.com
www.worldcat.org
http://ecclerk.erie.gov
www.maps.google.com
www.upgs.wordpress.com/2008/02/12/wheres-your-ancestral-village
http://boards.rootsweb.com/requestboard.aspx
www. rootsweb.ancestry.com/~alwalker/Codicil.htm

While the author has made every effort to provide accurate Internet addresses at the time of publication, neither the Publisher nor the author assume any responsibility for errors, or for changes that occur after publication. Furthermore, the Publisher does not have any control over and does not assume any responsibility for author or third party Web sites or their content.

If you find a site that is no longer available, check the Internet Archive by using their Wayback Machine to search for an archival copy of it. *www.archive.org*

While not mentioned in the text, Google's translation tools are helpful. The Google Toolbar offers a translation button for your browser. The Google translation Web page allows you to enter text, a Web page URL, or upload a document for translation. *www. toolbar.google.com* and *www.translate.google.com*

Addendum

Excerpt from Jewish Records Indexing - Poland (JRI-Poland)

The goal of Jewish Records Indexing - Poland (JRI-Poland) is to create searchable online indices of Jewish records from current and former territories of Poland. Where such records are available, they may include towns that are now part of Lithuania, Ukraine, and Belarus. Founded over ten years ago, the project was an outgrowth of Stanley Diamond's need for broad-based access to the Jewish vital records of the former Łomża Gubernia for genetic research purposes. A board of volunteers manages JRI-Poland. Indices in JRI-Poland come from two major sources: Indexing LDS microfilmed records, comprising about 2,000 films from more than 500 towns and villages and the JRI-Poland/Polish State Archives Project. These generally cover the last 25-35 years of the 19th century, when many grandparents and great-grandparents lived in Poland. To supplement information in vital records or substitute other sources for towns whose records are missing, JRI-Poland now includes a growing number of additional types of records. These range from: *Księgi/Spis Ludności (Books of Residents)*; census records; army draft lists; indices to burials in cemeteries and gravestone files; Polish passports; ghetto death records; birth, marriage, and death announcements in newspapers in Poland; and court and legal announcements in official newspapers (Monitor Polski). Warsaw-based professionals, funded by researchers around the world, do indexing of records in Poland. It is a model for indexing projects worldwide. ***www.jewishgen.org/jri-pl***

Excerpt from The Posen-L Mailing List

The Posen-L Mailing List was established in 1998 by James Birkholz. Posen-L is for anyone with a genealogical interest in the former Prussian province of Posen, Germany, now known as Poznań, Poland. In addition to supplying a forum, Posen-L strives to discuss in depth the history, the industry, the transportation and many other aspects of life in former times. Birkholz also maintains the Posen-L Web site which hosts a database of the *Churches of the Archdiocese of Gniezno and Poznań listed by Deaneries (Brevis Descriptio Historico-Geographica Ecclesiarum Archidioecesis Gnesnensis et Posnaniensis ad Ordinem Decanatuum Digestarum)* by Jan Korytkowski. The value of this 1888 work is that it lists all the small towns that were affiliated with each Catholic Church at the time. Once the appropriate church is identified, a researcher can proceed to check for available microfilms at the Family History Library. This database was created by Joseph Martin and Judith Zack to assist researchers seeking to locate a parish church in the Posen province where their ancestors' records might be located. ***www.posen-l.com***

HalGal

Matthew Bielawa's Web site provides general information on Halychyna/Eastern Galicia, a region that is often misunderstood or ignored in North America. Galicia was a northeastern province of the Austro-Hungarian Empire. It was located in what is now southeastern Poland and part of Ukraine. This site should be the starting point for anyone researching their ancestral roots in Western Ukraine/Eastern Galicia. Many of the pages will also be useful for Polish researchers of Western Galicia. *www.halgal.com*

Nationwide Index of Marriages Prior to 1899

The present site is devoted to the area of Russian Poland once known as the Duchy of Warsaw. Records from the Free City of Kraków created under Napoleon's Civil Code are included. *www.przodkowie.com/metryki/en.php*

The Poznań Project

Łukasz Bielecki's Poznań Project was developed as a way to resolve a problem common to many genealogists researching this area. The 19th century immigration and census records rarely provide the precise origin for people who left the Poznań/Posen province to settle in America, Australia, or elsewhere. The short label Posen is usually all that is provided confusing researchers who do not know if they should search the city of Posen or a village in the province of Posen. Volunteers are extracting marriage records spanning 1820-1889 for all the parishes of the region. *http://bindweed.man.poznan.pl/posen/search.php*

Pomeranian Genealogical Association

The Pomorskie Towarzystwo Genealogiczne (PTG) (Pomeranian Genealogical Association) was founded by a group of amateur genealogists who met each other via online discussion groups. They own photocopies of many church records from the Pomeranian area which were photographed in the Diocese Archives and parishes. PTG members are creating indexes of birth, marriage, and death records to publish on their Web site. *www.ptg.gda.pl*

GenPol

Tomasz Nitsch has launched a new web tool entitled GenBaza. This module is used to exchange information between genealogists with the help of geographic coordinates. Nitsch is a leading genealogist in Poland and has presented in the United States at the United Polish Genealogical Societies (UPGS) seminars and the Polish track for the National Genealogical Society (NGS). *www.genpol.com*

He has developed the list of Polish genealogical societies which follows:

- Polskie Towarzystwo Genealogiczne *www.genealodzy.pl*

- Bydgoskie Towarzystwo Heraldyczno-Genealogiczne *www.mok.bydgoszcz.pl/index.php?cid=199*

- KPTG Kujawsko - Pomorskie Towarzystwo Genealogiczne *www.kptg.pl*

- Lubelskie Towarzystwo Genealogiczne *www.ltg.pl*

- Lubuskie Towarzystwo Genealogiczne *www.ltg.zg.pl*

- Małopolskie Towarzystwo Genealogiczne *www.mtg-malopolska.org.pl*

- Związek Szlachty Polskiej *www.szlachta.org*

- Opolskie Towarzystwo Genealogiczne *www.otg.mojeforum.net*

- Ostrowskie Towarzystwo Genealogiczne *www.otg.net.pl*

- Suwalskie Towarzystwo Genealogiczne *www.mem.net.pl/stg*

- Śląskie Towarzystwo Genealogiczne *gento.free.ngo.pl/towarzystwo/stg.htm*

- Świętokrzyskie Towarzystwo Genealogiczne "Świętogen" *www.genealodzy-kielce.pl*

- Towarzystwo Genealogiczne Centralnej Polsk *www.tgcp.pl*

- Towarzystwo Genealogiczne Ziemi Częstochowskiej *www.genealodzy.czestochowa.pl*

- Towarzystwo Genealogiczno-Heraldyczne w Poznaniu *www.tgh.friko.pl*

- Warszawskie Towarzystwo Genealogiczne *www.wtg.org.pl*

- Wielkopolskie Towarzystwo Genealogiczne "Gniazdo" *www.wtg-gniazdo.org*

- Polskie Towarzystwo Heraldyczne *www.dig.com.pl/pther*

- Stowarzyszenie Potomków Sejmu Wielkiego *www.sejmwielki.pl*

- Towarzystwo Bambrów Poznańskich *www.city.poznan.pl/bambrzy*

- Genealogu Draugija - Genealogical Association in Vilnius *www.genealogija.lt*

- Verein für Familienforschung in Ost-und Westpreußen *www.genealogienetz.de/vereine/VFFOW*

- Ethnographic Museums in Poland *www.skanseny.net*

Family historians may enjoy viewing the online sites of the regional outdoor museums, known as skansens, located throughout Poland:

- BMW w Osowiczach *www.bialostockiemuzeumwsi.pl*

- GPE w Chorzowie *www.skansen.chorzow.pl*

- KDPE w Kłóbce *www.gwarypolskie.uw.edu.pl*

- KPE we Wdzydzach *www.muzeum-wdzydze.gda.pl*

- MBL w Olsztynku *www.muzeumolsztynek.com.pl*

- MBL w Sankouk *www.skansen.mblsanok.pl*

- ME w Toruniu *www.etnomuzeum.pl*

- MKL w Kolbuszowej *www.muzeum.kolbuszowa.pl/indexeng.php*

- MKL w Osieku *www.muzeum.pila.pl/index_eng.html*

- MW w Markowej *www.markowa.art.pl*

- MWM w Sierpcu *www.mwmskansen.pl*

- MR w Ciechanowcu *www.muzeumrolnictwa.pl*

- MWK w Tokarni *www.mwk.com.pl*

- MWL w Lublinie *www.skansen.lublin.pl/en/1-al-historia.html*

- MWO w Opolu *www.muzeumwsiopolskiej.pl*

- MWR w Radomiu *www.muzeum-radom.pl*

- NPE w Wygielzowie *www.mnpe.pl*

- OBL w Szymbarku *www.gorlice.art.pl*

- OPE w Zubrzycy *www.orawa.eu/angielski.html*

- SK w Nowogrodzie *www.skansenkurpiowski.republika.pl*

- SL w Maurzycach *www.powiat.lowicz.pl/lang:2*

- SPE w Nowym Saczu *www.muzeum.sacz.pl/index.htm?lang=2*

- WPE e Dziekanowicach *www.lednicamuzeum.pl*

- ZK w Kadzidle *www.skansen.kurpie.com.pl*